The New
Scenery
Tips & Techniques

Selected by Kent Johnson

KALMBACH
BOOKS

Printed in the United States of America

02 03 04 05 06 07 08 09 10 11   10 9 8 7 6 5 4 3 2 1

Visit our website at
http://kalmbachbooks.com
Secure online ordering available

Publisher's Cataloging-in-Publication
(Provided by Quality Books, Inc.)

The new scenery tips & techniques / selected by Kent
    Johnson. — 1st ed.
       p. cm.
       New scenery tips and techniques
       ISBN 0-89024-621-1

       1. Railroads—Models. I. Johnson, Kent J., 1968–
    II. Title: New scenery tips and techniques

    TF197.N49 2002   625.1'9
                              QBI02-200564

Art director: Kristi Ludwig
Book design: Kory Beavers

The material in this book has previously appeared as articles in *Model Railroader* Magazine. Most are reprinted in their entirety and may include an occasional reference to an item elsewhere in the same issue or in a previous issue of the magazine.

CONTENTS

GROUNDCOVER

TREES

WATER

BACKDROPS

TIPS & TECHNIQUES

Groundcover

1 Glueshell scenery

Make flexible scenery from white glue and rags

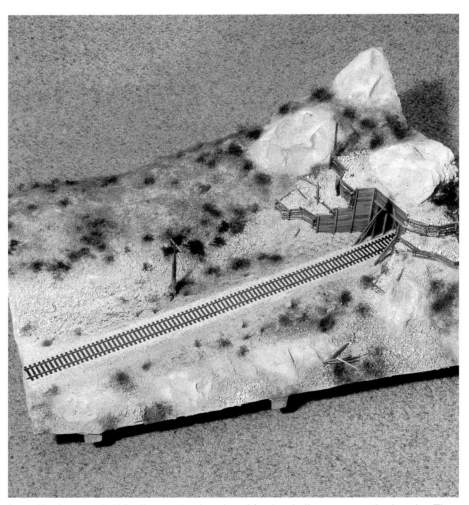

Leon Honings made this diorama to show how his glueshell scenery method works. The remaining photos show how he did it. Glueshell is flexible and withstands moves well.

BY LEON HONINGS
PHOTOS BY THE AUTHOR

My blood pressure used to go up each time I had to move my layout or drill holes for planting trees. Plaster is so brittle the hardshell would easily crack. Then, quite by chance, I discovered an alternative and a cure.

I noticed that the rags I used to clean my glue brushes became quite stiff when they dried. "Hey!" I thought, "Why not soak pieces of cloth in white glue instead of plaster?" A few hours later, I had a shell that was light, strong yet flexible, and wouldn't crack. I've used the glueshell method ever since.

This method has many advantages, and, as far as I can tell, no real drawbacks. You can work quickly with glueshell—you don't have to spend lots of time mixing batches of plaster. There's no plaster mess or Styrofoam particles to be cleaned up. And best of all, it's easy. If I can do it, anyone can!

What you need

The two basic ingredients for your glueshell are, of course, glue

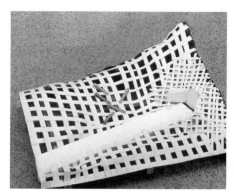

Fig. 1 SCENERY SUBSTRUCTURE. The cardboard webbing method, often used with hardshell, works with glueshell, too. Leon glues his strips together, clamping the joints with clothespins until the glue dries. Staples are equally effective.

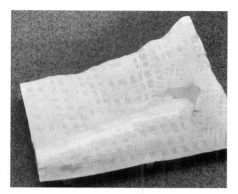

Fig. 2 BUILDING THE SHELL IN PLACE. Only one layer of glue-soaked rags is needed for the glueshell, but multiple layers can be used for added support in areas where plaster rocks will be added.

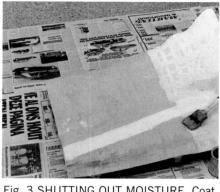

Fig. 3 SHUTTING OUT MOISTURE. Coat the shell with high-gloss lacquer to seal it. For the diorama seen in the photo, Leon sealed the bottom as well for added protection during transportation.

(common white glue is perfect) and cloth. I prefer plain white cotton bed sheets so I'm not distracted by colors or patterns while I study the shapes of my new hills and mountains.

Unless your layout is tiny, you'll want to buy the glue in bulk. You'll also need paint to seal your shell (I've found that glossy paint works better than flat). It's a good idea to keep a towel and a bucket of clean water handy just in case you have to answer the phone while you're building scenery.

Before going to work, put some newspaper on the floor to protect your carpet and cover all your trackwork with masking tape.

Tear the cloth into pieces about the size of your hand. Some pieces should be even smaller; you can use them in those places where the big ones won't fit. Don't cut the rags with scissors, as the sharp edges will be more difficult to hide. The ragged edges that result from tearing become almost invisible when covered by a layer or two of paint and ground foam.

Soak and mold

This is the fun part. I'll assume you have a subshell in place, such as cardboard webbing. See fig. 1. Make sure to use narrow strips to

get smooth transitions. About an inch wide is perfect.

Moisten a piece of cloth so it will accept the glue more easily, then submerge it into the glue and squeeze out the excess. Unfold the rag and lay it on your web. Repeat with a second cloth, laying it next to the first, and making sure there's a generous overlap. Continue until the web is completely covered. See fig. 2.

Let the shell dry for a few hours, then seal the surface with paint, as seen in fig. 3. Glossy lacquer works best because its surface is smoother and less penetrable. If you don't seal the surface, your shell will weaken when you add scenery material with water-based paints and adhesives.

The magic mix

Coat the shell with tan latex paint and sprinkle on ground foam while the latex is still wet. When the paint is completely dry, you can add a second layer of ground foam, using a mix of 45 percent water, 45 percent RTV (room temperature vulcanizing rubber) and 10 percent household ammonia.

I call this solution the Magic Mix because the RTV will remain flexible, no matter how many applications you need. The same can't be

said for matte medium or white glue. Wet the surface thoroughly, just as if you were using diluted matte medium.

Sometimes you need smooth ground cover, like plain dirt or sand. In such a case, the edges of the rags will cause trouble because they'll show. This problem had me stuck for a while, but I found a solution in an unlikely place.

I never thought I would cover parts of my layout with the filling from diapers, but I have. Mix the paper stuffing from disposable diapers with the solution of RTV/water/ammonia and stir it well. Apply a generous layer of this mix to your glueshell, smooth it out, and wait for a few days. When the pulp is dry, sand it to remove any rough spots. The shell should still be flexible. You can now add your favorite dirt material.

That's all there is to it. I think the glueshell method offers a nice alternative to conventional hardshell scenery, especially if a layout has to be moveable. And there's no waste. Since I started using glueshell, I've wondered why anyone would want to use plaster scenery at all. One thing's certain: I know I won't be going back.

2 Scenery in an afternoon

Sixteen square feet of plaster N scale desert blooms in less than 3 hours

BY BILL PEARCE
PHOTOS BY THE AUTHOR

After you've been a model railroader for a little while, you've likely noticed that some of your modeling friends have layouts that progress on almost a weekly basis, while others seem to be stuck in the plywood and track stage forever. Although this is to some extent the result of time constraints, it can also be the result of methods used.

One modeler might spend weeks with a dental pick over a single rock formation, while another has a technique that allows him to form miles of rock formations in an evening.

David Haines is one of the latter. His N scale Raton Pass layout that appeared in the 60th anniversary issue of *Model Railroader* (January 1994) was in the dumpster only a few months later.

Today, his new and improved version sports nearly complete basic

David Haines scenicked this 4 x 4-foot section of his N scale layout in an afternoon. The following steps will show you how to make scenery like this efficiently.

scenery. How he got from an empty room to this state is the result of techniques that make efficient use of his modeling time.

Here's David's technique for quick basic scenery. The photos show an area about 4 by 4 feet. Multiple layers of Hydrocal plaster have already been applied over alu-

minum window screen, giving a smooth surface unblemished by cardboard ribs.

We'll go from plaster to finish in about three hours. Of course, you'll need to have all your supplies ready ahead of time. Now get your stopwatches ready—it's time to start!

12:15 p.m. Use a hand sprayer to dampen the plaster, as dry Hydrocal will absorb moisture like a sponge, making the paint dry too fast. The hole will accommodate David's cattle pen from his previous layout.

12:20 p.m. Paint the white plaster a basic earth color of thinned latex paint, about 1 part paint to 2 parts water. This will add color and serve as an adhesive for the first layer of ground foam. The shade used depends on the geographic area you model. Liberally coat areas that will remain bare earth or grassy, avoiding roads and building sites.

12:35 p.m. The initial layer of texture is next. For this area of New Mexico, David used Woodland Scenics fine Mixed Grass. With a tea strainer, sprinkle a light layer over the wet paint. It's not necessary to cover all the paint thoroughly. Let some basic earth color show through for bare ground. For more vertical areas, blow foam onto the paint.

1:05 p.m. Lightly sprinkle coarse foam on the dampened area. David used a total of five colors from Woodland Scenics and AMSI. Variety is the key. Duplicate nature with a subtle mix of colors and random placement. Then, using an old paintbrush, sweep the foam off roads and anywhere else it shouldn't be. After all, we don't want grass growing out of concrete and asphalt, do we?

2:30 p.m. We're almost done! The kind of low brush that's so common in New Mexico is easily duplicated with Woodland Scenics foam clusters. Pull off random-sized chunks and dip them into a jar of the same diluted white glue, using tweezers. Again, mixing colors, place them in groups or individually as appropriate.

1:00 p.m. The area is then sprayed with rubbing alcohol. This acts as a wetting agent and is more effective than wet water (water with a few drops of dishwashing detergent added). The obvious advantage of the method David is using is that you don't have to wait for materials to dry before moving on to the next step.

1:50 p.m. To make sure everything stays put, mix diluted white glue, about 1 part glue to 2 parts water. White glue doesn't dilute well, but warm water makes it easier. A few drops of detergent or Photo-Flo also help. Spray everything with glue till it's sopping wet. Direct it so as little foam as possible is displaced. Add more foam to replace any that washed away, then lightly spray everything with rubbing alcohol.

3:00 p.m. You're finished! Go down to the local hobby shop and tell the guys how sharp you are. This really isn't the end, of course. After the area dries overnight, you can complete the scene with trees, telephone poles, and roads. Additional details are a never-ending part of our hobby, but this base scenery is a big step toward completion.

3 Fake fur grass

Add grassy fields to your layout

BY KEN PATTERSON
PHOTOS BY THE AUTHOR

When our club, the Midwest Valley Modelers, was planning scenes for our modular layout, we knew we needed to include the grassy fields typical of the Midwest. We also needed to find a method of modeling these fields that would be simple but produce good-looking results.

We found the answer to our problem in Eric Bronsky's "Modeling tall prairie grass" in the March 1985 issue of *Model Railroader*. Eric used fake fur, a synthetic material used in making toy stuffed animals. We adopted many of his techniques and added a few touches of our own.

The fake fur can be found in fabric and craft stores. It comes in an assortment of colors. The greens tend to be a little vivid, so I prefer to start with light tan or brown and then use an airbrush to paint it the desired shade of green. Follow the step-by-step photos, and it won't be long before tall grassy fields threaten to overrun your right-of-way.

Ken Patterson made the realistic wild grass from fake fur. It looks just like the tall, wild grasses found alongside railroads throughout the country.

1. Once the basic landform is complete, Ken brushes on a liberal coating of Liquid Nails adhesive and presses the fake fur into place. He waits overnight to be sure the adhesive sets completely before proceeding.

2. Ken trims the material with a pair of sharp scissors. For the best results, he varies the height of the strands. Trimming the fur down to the nap in some places forms realistic bare patches between clumps of grass.

3. After using scissors to trim the fake fur, Ken found an electric hair clipper was much faster and far easier on his knuckles. This is now his "weapon of choice" when trimming large areas.

4. Tan or brown fur makes good dead grass, but for a summer scene Ken airbrushes the fur. Alternating between yellow and green produces a realistic blend of colors. Be sure to do this in a well-ventilated area.

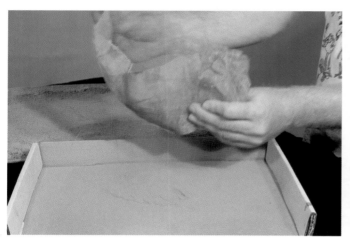

5. Ken uses fine plumbing screen, available from Ace Hardware, to sift ordinary dirt. This material is much finer than window screen.

6. Once he's sifted the dirt, Ken dumps it onto the "grass." Neatness doesn't count at this stage. Once he completes the next step, it will look like the grass is growing out of the dirt.

7. Ken uses an old hairbrush to move the dirt until the grass looks like it's growing out of the earth. Then he bonds it in place with a 50:50 mixture of glue and water, applying it with a mist sprayer or contact lens cleaner bottle.

4 Add weeds to your layout

Start with inexpensive twine from your hardware store

BY SAM SWANSON
PHOTOS BY THE AUTHOR

Ever looked at trackside scenes and felt something was missing? It's weeds! Big bushy weeds! Take a look at any real railroad's right-of-way and you'll see what I mean.

You can make miniature weeds from many materials, but I prefer the appearance of natural fiber. Jute and sisal twine are available at low cost in most hardware stores. See fig. 1. The thin-stranded jute twine is ideal to simulate field grass and bushes, while the thick-stranded sisal twine works best for reeds and wide-bladed grass. Avoid the glossy synthetic twines, as they're too uniform in size and the strands are difficult to color.

Coloring the twine

Start your weed production by cutting 2″ lengths of twine and placing them on a sheet of typing paper, as shown in fig. 2. I stain the cut twine with thin washes of enamel and acrylic paints. Some washes match the color of my ground cover, while others are liberally and randomly streaked with dark or light greens, browns, and yellows. Experiment here until you arrive at several appealing color combinations to use on your layout.

Let the colored twine dry several hours and loosen any stuck-together fibers by rolling the twine between your thumb and index finger. (If you can't break the twine into individual fibers, you've used too much paint.) Stained jute twine is the starting point for the three weeds I use most: tufts of grass, leafy and flowering bushes, and ivy. Examples of all three are in fig. 3.

Weed production

Tufts of grass are the easiest to make and "plant." Cut ¼″ bits of colored twine, dip one end into

Fig. 1 NATURAL FIBER TWINE. Hardware stores sell jute and sisal twine in handy pocket packs, but the author also finds discards in fields and alongside rural roads.

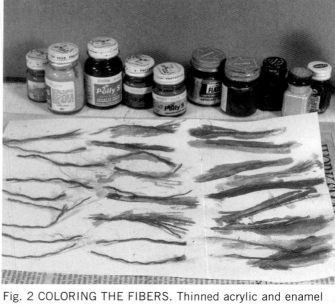

Fig. 2 COLORING THE FIBERS. Thinned acrylic and enamel hobby paints are used to stain the short lengths of twine in a variety of green, yellow, and brown colors.

Fig. 3 WEED SHAPES. Tufts of stained jute twine can be shaped into ivy, grass, and leafy or flowering bushes, while sisal twine works best to simulate reeds in swampy areas.

Fig. 4 FOLIAGE. It's easy to add leaves or flowers to bushes by painting the ends of the jute tuft with Testor's Dullcote and then dipping the miniature plant in ground foam.

white glue, then roll the end between your thumb and index finger to form a point as the glue sets. Tease the individual fibers apart with tweezers to produce a bushy appearance. The tuft is now ready for planting as grass or transformation into a bush.

For a bush, you'll need some ground foam and a bottle of Testor's Dullcote. I use Woodland Scenics Blended Turf as leaves and the Flowers assortment for the flowering bushes. Just brush the twine fibers with Dullcote and dip them into a pile of foam. Repeat this step until you're satisfied with the density of the leaves or flowers.

Similarly, leafy and flowering ivy can be made by twisting jute fibers into a branching vine shape and tacking them in place with white glue. Brush the tops of the vines with Dullcote and dip them into medium or coarse ground foam to simulate the leaves.

Planting

Install the ivy by gluing it to the base of the structure and securing the individual vines with white glue.

Plant tufts of grass and bushes by making a small hole in your layout's terrain using an awl. Dip the plant in white glue and insert it in the hole.

Next time you're out, take a close look at how the different weeds tend to grow in clumps. With twine and ground foam, you can produce a similar variety of weeds to enhance your railroad's right-of-way.

11

5 Fat-fat fibers

Carpet fibers make a fast and inexpensive ground cover

BY JORY S. TETZLAFF
PHOTOS BY THE AUTHOR

Years ago, I remember hearing ads for a new carpet that announced: "Fat-fibers, fat-fat fibers by Kodel." I don't know whether any of today's carpets bear that trademark or even if that firm is still in business. What I do know is that almost all of them are composed of some artificial material: polyester, nylon, and so on. These synthetic fibers work great as ground cover and foliage material.

I found that out when I was trying to complete a fairly generous, empty section of terrain on my HO scale layout. It had become obvious that a relatively large investment would have to be made in the commercial scenery department. Hesitant to dig too deep into my pockets, I looked for alternative methods to finish the project.

Just a short time before we had several rooms in our home recarpeted. As the family's "pack rat," I had saved several of the larger pieces of cutoffs and scrap material. You've probably already guessed—they were the answer to my scenery problem. Here I'll explain how I used them and what other applications I've found for them.

In the lead photo you can see how I've used carpet for certain kinds of scenery.

If you like what you see there and think you want to give my technique a shot, you'll find what's necessary in fig. 1.

Materials

• Scrap carpet pieces. A short- to medium-length nap seems to work best. Color isn't real important, but

The vegetation growing at the base of this trestle on the author's layout was made out of carpet fibers. In this article he describes the materials and techniques he used.

Fig. 1. Here's everything that you'll need to turn carpet fibers into a scenery medium.

I'd advise sticking with earth tones (brown, beige, tan). These scraps are usually free for the asking at a flooring distributor.
• Utility knife.
• Sharp hand scissors. Cheap pairs don't work well, and neither do metal-cutting shears. And don't steal your wife's sewing pair. You'll

avoid a lot of hollering if you buy a pair of your own.
• Aerosol spray paints. Glossy or flat is fine. Just get a couple of greens and a light yellow.
• Ground foam. Again, greens, browns, and a yellow are necessary. Very fine sawdust, if you have some, will work in place of the yellow.

Fig. 2. First cut the carpet into strips 4" to 5" wide, then cut the strips into small squares. Always cut through the carpet's backing.

Fig. 3. Next, carefully shear the nap from the backing with sharp hand scissors. A dull pair or metal-cutting shears won't work as well.

Fig. 4. To convert the fibers into a soft and fluffy mass, rapidly agitate them between your fingers or work them against a tabletop.

Fig. 5. Only a small portion of the nap resists unraveling. Don't worry about that, as it will get lost in the finished scenery.

Procedure

With all the materials handy, we're ready to convert the carpet into a useful form (look at figs. 2 through 6 as you go). A few words of caution: Use extreme care when cutting with the utility knife; also, cut through the backing and not the nap side. Laying the piece on an old sheet of lightweight wood will prevent any damage to good surfaces. Oh yes, fingers cut easily! Be careful!

After you've sliced the larger pieces into strips about 4" to 5" wide, cut each one into smaller, more manageable squares as shown in fig. 2. That way you'll be able to use the scissors more efficiently than if you're working with an oversize section.

Next, shear the nap from each square (fig. 3). Run in with the scissors close to the backing. Take your time, and be sure your scissors are sharp. It will be rough going if they're dull.

Once the shearing is complete, the most difficult part of the work is finished. But to make best use of the nap, it should be turned into a fluffy sort of mass by gently agitating it between your fingers (fig. 4).

When all but about 10 percent or so has unraveled, it's ready for installation (fig. 5). As for the strands of fibers not unraveled, they'll get lost in the finished product by adding additional texture and depth.

Installation and coloring

Trial and error has taught me that it's most productive to install the fibers as-is where they'll go and to work from there. I haven't mentioned adhesives for two reasons. First, they aren't always necessary. The lightweight yet slightly coarse fibers tend to cling well to surfaces, particularly plaster scenery. Second, the spray paints used as the basic coloring agent serve as the adhesive for both the fibers and toppings. Still, if you want more permanence, white glue or any brand of spray adhesive will work well.

Figure 6 shows how I've placed the fibers in position on a relatively steep embankment without an adhesive. The first step is to give the fibers a base color using any of the shades of green. Combining different shades adds shadow and depth and eliminates monotony.

Immediately follow with a dusting of various ground foams. Use darker shades of foam first, then add a spit or two of light green and yellow to enhance detail. The key to success is to apply both paints and foams very lightly. "A little dab will do ya!" Otherwise you'll end up with far too dense a mass.

You may wonder why I don't use carpets with straight shades, green in particular. Without getting too technical, let me note that most carpets are composed of various primary colors to produce a given shade. The primary colors tend to be too loud and produce poor scenery, looking more "globbish" than lacy.

You can, however, easily alter

Fig. 6. After installing the fibers, the author gives them a light base coat of spray paint. Then he dusts on several shades of ground foam.

Fig. 7. Any remaining scraps can be used for hedgerows and other ground cover, as is shown here on his layout.

tones and hues by combining different shades of fibers and paints. Or you can try eliminating the paint and using a spray adhesive, followed by ground foam. I prefer the paint/foam method, as it gives me more control over the end result.

Other uses

Hold it, don't throw away those scraps from the scraps. Good use can be made of them in other areas. Narrow strips of carpet, backing and all, can be painted and dusted with ground foams right at the workbench to make excellent renditions of hedgerow plantings (fig. 7).

Larger pieces of material can be prepared in the same manner to represent meadows and low rolling hills. Final detailing, trees, shrubs, fence rows, and the like will put the icing on the cake.

A medley of variations is possible using carpet fibers as a scenery medium. I've been pleased with the overall results.

Furthermore, I've found this to be a successful way to scenick dioramas, module setups, and portable layouts. Because of the nature of the material, it is virtually immune to decay, dryness, and dampness.

Now back to business. Just how many square yards did you say you needed for that rec room? Psst, stick with earth tones. . . .

6 Western scenery

How-tos for handling the subtleties of arid scenery in foreground locations

BY PAT GERSTLE
PHOTOS BY THE AUTHOR

Many modelers are drawn to Western scenery: snow-capped mountain ranges, twisting canyons, endless deserts, and pine forests. I suspect some modelers even choose the location before they choose a railroad. The photo of Clear Creek Canyon, Colo. (fig. 1), is the sort of scene that inspires us to model the West, but what we usually see when standing trackside, as fig. 2 shows, is a few feet of rocky soil, some scrubby bushes, and maybe some larger rocks and a hillside behind the train. This article is about how to

Fig. 1 CLEAR CREEK CANYON. This view typifies the scenery of the West, but few layouts have the space to model such large vistas.

Fig. 2 TRACKSIDE SCENERY. At trackside, you rarely see big vistas; usually you see a relatively shallow scene of rocks and grass.

Fig. 3 BASE TERRAIN. After shaping the basic landform and adding rock castings, Pat paints the whole area a light tan.

Fig. 4 ROCKS AND MORE ROCKS. Woodland Scenics talus and ballast provide a wide range of rock sizes to work with.

Fig. 5 PLANT LIFE. Plants don't dominate Western scenery, but they're needed. Concentrate them where water naturally collects.

model this up-close-to-the-action trackside detail.

Research

Among my primary references for colors and general scenes are pictures from railroad wall calendars. The photos are large, very high quality, and provide a detailed view of the railroad and its surroundings. I have an equally large collection of personal photographs. For general how-to on scenery, I recommend Dave Frary's *How to Build Realistic Scenery for Model Railroads* from Kalmbach Publishing.

Terrain

In fig. 3, 1 have cut and glued some 2″-thick blue foam to form the base of a small rise on which a mine will be placed. I have covered the foam with plaster-soaked towels or gauze. I then painted this base with a soupy mix of plaster to fill in any holes and thin areas. Next I added

rock castings, fixing them in place with plaster and painting around them with the plaster soup to blend them into the base. Finally, without waiting for the plaster to dry, I painted the ground and castings with the base color.

Western scenery is mostly beige with some light tans and reds thrown in. I use Sears no. 770 interior flat latex diluted with an equal amount of water. Brush it over everything except the rocks. On the rocks, mix one part paint with two parts water for more of a stain. Now wait for things to dry, then brush on some dilute raw umber for reddish highlights. Finish with your favorite black wash (either very thin black paint or India ink and alcohol) to bring out the details. Your finished scene should look something like fig. 3.

Ground cover

The next process introduces most of the surface details, and

most of the surface detail in the West consists of **LOTS** of rocks, of all sizes, scattered and piled everywhere. I used the following Woodland Scenics products: talus (fine, medium, coarse, and extra coarse in Buff and Brown; ballast (fine and medium) in Buff and Brown; turf and coarse turf in Yellow Grass, Burnt Grass, Earth, and Soil; clump foliage in Burnt Grass, Light Green, and Fall Mix; and field grass in Natural Straw, Harvest Gold, and Light Green.

I also use finely sifted dirt and goldmine tailings I gathered from the area I'm modeling. I make a palette of these materials by placing them in empty tuna cans in a box lid.

Start by painting a small area (about 1 square foot) with a thick coat of full-strength white glue. Now drop the large talus pieces randomly and in groups over the area. If the area is sloped, place more toward the bottom. Next, drop the medium talus around, followed by the fine. Use more of the medium and lots more of the fine. Put some of the medium and fine talus around the large and randomly distribute the rest over the whole area. Concentrate the talus in gullies, stream beds, and at the base of rock formations. At this stage your scene should look like fig. 4.

Now scatter small patches of the turf and grass around—not a lot, and concentrated in the areas where moisture would collect. To fix the groundcover, I spray on a coat of "wet water" (water with one or two drops of dish detergent added so that it soaks into the groundcover). Then I use an eyedropper to distribute a 50/50 mixture of white glue and water. Make sure the ground is thoroughly saturated with glue.

Only when all is solidly dry do I plant the larger shrubs and trees. The shrubs are clump foliage and the trees are pines and aspens from K&S Scenery Products. A lot of the shrubs are placed near the larger rocks because moisture collects in the shadows.

The last thing I add is the field grass—I love this stuff! I add clumps in all shapes and sizes around larger rocks and in gullies. I think by striving for realism in the area you would see up close I've captured the look of Western scenery without trying to include the snow-capped back range!

7 Modeling a "rainscape"

Some contrast for your layout's sunny scenes

A dramatic rainstorm coming across the mountains provides an exciting backdrop against the movement of trains.

BY RAND HOOD
PHOTOS BY THE AUTHOR

My train crews have been conditioned to expect bright, cheerful sunshine to warm them as they work. It's no wonder that when they hit rain on the tortuous 2 percent grind up to Moffat Tunnel, their little scale moods turn as gloomy as the surrounding weather. Modeling a "rainscape," a scene representing a rain shower, builds contrast into a layout and adds to the illusion of trains covering more distance and time.

Calm before the storm

Start by building ditches along the railroad and having them drain into adjacent streams. Make the ditches slightly deeper than normal, as they'll be filled with scenic materials. Once you've completed the plaster shell and tinted all the rockwork, paint dark latex earth color (see the chart for all the formulas) over the landscape.

Sift real dirt onto the paint. Then, with a spray bottle of "wet" water, water with a few drops of dishwashing detergent added, saturate everything so the paint mixes and tints the soil. This also creates some natural water erosion. Allow this to dry overnight.

Paint a wash of water-course tint along all of the waterways and erosion areas as shown in fig. 1. Allow the tint to dry, then seal the waterways by brushing them with a coat of full-strength acrylic gloss medium.

Let it rain

Apply ballast to the track and spread rocky soil along the road-

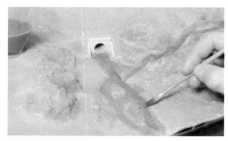

Fig. 1. WATERWAYS. The darkest colors in the rainscape are the waterways.

Fig. 2. THE WET LOOK The tinted gloss medium creates a rainy, wet appearance on the scenery.

Fig. 3. CREEK The creek bed flows rapidly because of extra water from ditches and runoff.

Fig. 4. RAINFALL. The vertical streaks on the backdrop make it look like a rainfall is coming.

Fig. 5. LIGHTNING. Carefully cut the lightning bolt from the back side of the backdrop.

bed edges and in the waterways. Wet the entire landscape and apply ground foam, using bright greens along the waterways and yellower tones on the open slopes. Rewet the landscape and use a squeeze bottle to apply the tinted gloss medium, soaking everything until it's milky white. Give rock faces a coat of the mix as well.

When this has dried, everything will have a slight sheen and the extra tint will deepen and blend the landscape, as fig. 2 shows. Re-apply the mix if you desire a deeper tone. Apply any delicate foliage, such as clumps of grass fibers placed in individual holes, and add telephone poles, lineside details, and trees to complete the scene. Add a clear acrylic finishing spray over the scene to add some raindrop sparkles.

Using the Enviro-Tex mixture and a small disposable brush, paint the ditches intermittently near the top slopes and solidly in the downslope areas to simulate the water collecting and running.

Pour puddles anywhere water may collect, and vary the watercourse width. The longer a ditch runs, the more water it must shed, so its drainage point will either be very wide or narrow and full.

When the Enviro-Tex has almost cured, tease it with a toothpick to create rolling water around stones and logs. The river should run with force, as shown in fig. 3. After the water has completely cured, highlight waves and cascades with full-strength gloss medium tinted with white acrylic paint.

Backdrop

The most important element to lending believability to the rainscape is the backdrop. Fortunately, it's easy to render a stormy, rain-streaked sky. If you choose to back-light the scene, use .040" styrene for the backdrop. Styrene can be purchased in 4 x 8-foot sheets from plastics dealers.

Using adequate ventilation, spray both sides of the sheet with gray enamel primer to provide a base for the acrylic paint and to keep light from shining through when it's backlit. Working in 6-foot sections, cover the entire backdrop with light sky color.

With the paint still wet, use a 3″ brush to "scumble," or scrub randomly, the dark gray sky mix into the base paint. The resulting mixing and streaking produce surprisingly realistic clouds. Keep the paint wet by misting water over the surface.

Lightly fan all the cloud forms with a dry 3″ brush to soften the edges. Simulate falling rain by brushing random vertical strokes through the clouds, and concentrate strokes directly underneath certain clouds to yield heavy rainfall, as shown in fig. 4.

Next, scumble a land mass into the wet background using the light landscape mix. The result should be soft and streaky. Pull a few rain strokes over the horizon with the dry brush, and instantly a sky of believable depth appears. Scumble the dark landscape mix over the foreground, rendering vague suggestions of form rather than detail. Once the paint dries completely, you can make minor adjustments by using matte medium and color tints.

Lightning strikes

Trace a simple lightning bolt onto paper, then transfer it to the backdrop underneath an ominous-looking cloud. Using a Dremel no. 111 etching bit and a motor tool set on slow speed, carefully cut out the bolt, as shown in fig. 5. Apply "lightning filler" with a toothpick into the lightning void. This will dry transparent and stabilize the opening. To backlight the lightning, use a low-wattage bulb and keep the light source away from the surface.

Overhead fluorescent fixtures provide an even, shadowless light source for the rainscape. Gray gels with 25 and 50 percent transparency, available at camera stores, can be taped over the fixture's diffuser covering. This soft light blends the entire scene into a rainy atmosphere.

A rainscape is an easy addition to existing scenery and breaks the sunshine monopoly we tend to build into our layouts. Drop a thunderstorm cassette into your tape player, flip on the lightning, and watch your scale figures scamper for cover. Oh well, as they say, into everyone's life . . .

8 Let it snow!
Modeling winter on the Red Wing

BY MELANIE BUELLESBACH
PHOTOS BY BILL ZUBACK

Most years the staff of *Model Railroader* builds a project layout to be completed in September. Then it goes on the road to several train shows in the Midwest around the holidays. Last year we refreshed our old 4 x 8 Red Wing project layout instead. Since 1994, the Red Wing had been on display at Kalmbach and had collected quite a layer of dirt and dust. The scenery, including all the trees, had seen better days and would have to be redone.

Then came a better idea: cover the Red Wing with snow.

Just as the real white stuff covers the browning grass and gives a fresh look to the outdoors, our modeled snow would cover the aging scenery and hide imperfections that had developed on the structures and some of the track. It would also give a whole new look to a layout people had seen before.

Time was short, so I made it up as I went along. Fortunately, having grown up in Wisconsin, I didn't need to research typical winter scenes or learn what snow drifts look like. But covering 32 square feet with snow is no small task.

First storm of the season

My first job was to remove the chunks of ground foam scenery and trees. I used a putty knife, my

Ice skaters on the HO scale Red Wing layout enjoy their gloss medium rink, while in the background the milling company must have a Saturday shift, since the snowplow is hurriedly clearing the parking lot.

Our project layout, as built in 1994, had a bit more foliage on it than it does now.

Bill of materials

Accurate Dimensionals
13 snow, shimmering (3)

E-R Model Importers
120 Santa Claus

Faller
1464 assorted fir trees

IHC
8852 winter people

Life-Like
1654 dump trucks (2)

Preiser figures
10117 standing pedestrians
10310 family Krause in winter
10312 skiing long distance
10315 skaters
14005 boys and girls in winter
   clothing
14007 children in winter clothes
14136 shopping

Roco
1775 truck snowplow

Trident
90103 Federal Express delivery van

Woodland Scenics
140 soft flake snow shaker (9)

Miscellaneous
lightweight spackling compound
isopropyl rubbing alcohol
Elmer's white glue

bare hands, and a bit of force. After I'd dusted off the buildings, a Shop-Vac removed remaining bits of ground foam and dirt.

And then it snowed. It snowed nine bottles of Woodland Scenics snow. I started with the hillside, sprinkling on the snow, soaking it with a spray of isopropyl rubbing alcohol, then drizzling on a 50/50 mix of white glue and water. After covering all the formerly green areas and all the track but the main line with the white stuff, I let it dry.

The snow wasn't very deep; in fact it looked like a mid-winter thaw was under way. So I covered everything with another layer, mixing some Accurate Dimensionals shimmering snow into the top coat to give the snow sparkle.

Soaking the snow with alcohol is important because it allows the glue to penetrate. If the glue dries on top, the snow will eventually crack, revealing loose powder

underneath. For the same reason applying two thin layers of snow is better than one thick one.

Starting off with a green base worked well, because real snow falls on grass and bushes, and some green peeks through, especially from evergreens. It also gave the landscape texture.

The snowplows are out

A good Midwestern town like Red Wing has its streets cleared by sunrise; therefore I needed piled snow along the road sides and outer edges of the parking lots. Lightweight spackling compound, which has the consistency of cake frosting (I used the Red Devil One-time brand), makes great snow banks.

The trick is to drop it onto the general vicinity with a plastic spoon, let it set up for 10 to 15 minutes until it's

more workable and less likely to stick to your fingers, then sprinkle it with snow and form into piles.

Up on the rooftops

Next I went to work on the buildings. With literally a handful of spackling compound, I attacked as if I were a blizzard blowing in from the north. I smeared it on,

The Red Wing layout was transformed into a snowy winter scene to give it a different look and to revitalize it after six years on display.

sometimes wiping off the excess, in an attempt to realistically build up the snow on the same sides of each building as a storm would, leaving areas on the opposite sides untouched.

Playing in the snow

Typical winter scenes help draw people into the layout, so I added several. There are kids having a snowball fight by the firehouse: I made two snow forts from styrene, built up the snow around them, and added bundled-up children.

For the ice rink I began with a piece of styrene, painted on several layers of gloss medium, and built up the snow banks around it. Skaters, a warming shed, and fire completed the scene.

I put holiday shoppers in the streets, the omnipresent FedEx truck delivering last minute gifts, skiers gliding through the newly added pine trees, and sledders flying down the hill.

And what's outside nearly every store right before Christmas? The Salvation Army kettle, which I fashioned from scrap styrene rod and strips and painted red. I then added a three-man band playing carols.

I needed holiday decorations, and to no one's surprise the craft store had its Christmas supplies out in September. I found wreaths to hang on the water tower, red bows for the bridge, and Santa in a sleigh with his reindeer to perch on the milling company roof. No, they're not precisely to scale, but when you need Christmas decorations on short notice, you can't be too picky, and the overall impression worked well.

Will spring ever come?

A word of caution: Once it snows on your layout it'll always be winter. Several people who saw the display asked how we'd clean the tracks and structures off, and the answer is we won't.

The winterized Red Wing was a big hit at shows. Many people commented that just looking at it made them cold. And it was especially fun to see the kids discover the little details at their eye level—the snowball fight, snowplow, Santa on the roof, and the ice skaters—scenes they could relate to.

Whether you're looking to refresh an old layout or just add a winter scene, I hope I've given you helpful tips and shown what fun it can be.

9 Modeling a winterscape: Part 1
Painting a wintery backdrop and creating ice and snow

A sparkling blanket of white greets the helper crew exiting Moffat Tunnel. Geography isn't the only rugged feature on author Rand Hood's layout, as Mother Nature also deals a forceful hand against the railroad.

BY RAND HOOD
PHOTOS BY RAND AND KAREN HOOD

Winter is a season of austere beauty—a serene time when long, violet shadows streak fields of white, only to be scattered by the icy winds of an oncoming blizzard. I wanted to model such a winter scene on my HO scale Denver & Rio Grande layout, and I had the perfect spot for it, the valley lying outside the 9,000-foot-high Moffat Tunnel.

Now my layout features dramatically different scenes, and it's rewarding to watch trains traverse the elements as they move from sunny prairie through rain and cutting sleet until they finally reach the snow-laden valley. Adding these weathery transitions makes the trains appear to

Fig. 2 BRUSHES. Rand paints bare trees with a no. 4 fan brush, shown here. For background shadows he uses a no. 10 flat brush, and for pines he uses a no. 8 round.

travel farther. Also, operations have become more challenging with blizzards and snowslides to deal with.

The techniques for modeling a winterscape are not difficult. Let's explore the possibilities.

Winter palette

A wide range of cool grays, browns, and ochres can be seen in the vegetation and rocks. Bright yellows, icy lavenders, and deep purple-blues define the sky. All of these colors are heightened by the sharp contrast of the brilliant white snow.

I chose purple-blue clouds, backlit by a yellow sky, as the basis for my winterscape and worked these colors into a preliminary sketch.

"I'm no artist . . ."

Painting a backdrop can be intimidating, but it follows a logical pattern of mixing accurate colors to match your reference photos or sketches, then applying them in layers.

Here are two important guides: First, colors change tonally when placed next to other colors. What I thought was the perfect pine green mixed on the palette appeared too green against those deep blue clouds. I corrected this with a touch of blue and black. Second,

mixing more than four paints together results in color that is muddy and less energetic.

Colors and their purest blends are shown in fig. 1. They are listed in order, from the greatest amount of color needed first to trace amounts of paint last.

One rule to remember: Blue changes a color more rapidly than any other color by far, even in small amounts, so be careful.

Purchase a 6.75-ounce tube of white paint and smaller .67- or 2-ounce tubes of colors, and a no. 10 flat, no. 8 round, and no. 4 fan brush. Figure 2 illustrates their uses. For large areas use a 3″ house-painting brush.

Also, you'll need a 2½″ flexible palette knife with a rounded end. You can use it for mixing paint as well as creating snowdrifts.

When choosing paint, stay away from acrylics for painted skies because of their fast drying time. Instead, use oil alkyd artist's paint. With its day-long drying time, it's easier to add subtle cloud tints and soften the sky realistically. Mix oil paints with small amounts of Liquin painting medium and turpentine for a fluid paint. Alkyds dry to a semi-flat sheen that shimmers in scumbled (tight swirled) cloud brushstrokes, as shown in fig. 3. Sky color painted in direc-

tional strokes remains flat, heightening the effect of the clouds.

Getting started

Give the Masonite backdrop two coats of acrylic house primer tinted with acrylic phthalo blue to ensure a bright, cool base. Paint with a roller to provide an even surface.

Loosely sketch the horizon line with the yellow sky color. Keep the horizon above eye level if you're painting mountainous terrain. Sketch towering clouds colliding with the landscape. You can easily erase errant lines with turpentine. Paint in the sky with a large brush, leaving the interiors of the clouds uncovered. Cadmium orange blended into the upper sky will create the illusion of depth.

Fig. 3 CLOUDS. Using light, swirling brush strokes within clouds suggests shimmering light.

Fig. 4 WET-ON-WET METHOD. Painting foreground trees over a snowy background yields a frosty appearance. Cool cloud underpainting makes distant mountains recede.

Using a clean brush, swirl the bluish clouds lightly into the sky color until the two edges blend. Add an underpainting of cloud color where remote snowy mountains rise out of the landscape, then define them by overpainting with pure white. Controlling the amount of the two-color blend creates the mountain's form and makes the peaks recede far into the distance as shown in fig. 4.

Brush circular strokes of the cloud color, altered with lightened ultramarine red, into reflected light areas to separate the clouds into layers. This is shown in fig. 5. Trees then touched into the mountain will coolly fade in the distance.

Snowy landscapes

You can now use acrylics, as it's fine to cover oil paint with acrylics (but not vice versa). I continued with the alkyds mixed with oil painting medium 1 (a flattener), so large hillsides could be blended smoothly into shadow. Acrylics require smaller working surfaces to ensure smooth blending.

Paint sunny snow first, using white and a very light touch of cadmium yellow. Use a separate brush of light blue to create the sur-

rounding shadowy snow, then blend the snow edges together. Add highlighted snowbanks with hard lines of pure white against deeper blues.

Sunlight reflects powerfully off snow. Add tree and vegetation colors directly into the sunny snow and they'll appear over-illuminated. A few touches of light greenish yellow on sunward pine branches is very effective, as shown in fig. 6.

Let this dry before adding frostbitten trees to the shadowy terrain. When adding large tree masses you invariably run out of paint—mix an altered color to create different tree ridges in the forest.

Paint barren deciduous trees with the no. 4 fan brush, used vertically on edge in a drybrush manner. A couple of vertical swipes and a few random upward diagonals create a tangle of branches. Adding more blue to the tree mix adds shadows, and more yellowy ochre continues the streaking sunlight. Add each sparingly and don't overbrush or mix them together.

Add fine branch work, shown in fig. 7, by scratching the paint with the point of a palette knife, revealing the bluish primer. Drybrush

winter bushes and grasses with variants of the deciduous tree color to keep a harmony of subdued colors.

You can mix glazes or thin washes of transparent colors by adding more Liquin to oils and matte medium to acrylics. Use these to deepen interiors of shadows or to dull bright colors. Apply glazes after the base painting is completely dry, to avoid lifting the color underneath.

Snow selection

Vintage Reproductions offers an unparalleled range of surface snow products. Made of plastic crystals, fibers, and iridescent flakes, they come pre-mixed to represent various snow conditions, as shown in fig. 8.

For the deep snows of the Moffat area I selected the no. 772 Cold-Dry mixture. For receding snows, no. 771 Fluffy-Wet is the perfect choice. Bluish Slushy Snow, no. 773, is used to represent shadows and melting snow packs. These are all available with a microsparkle additive. Because the thousands of glittering flakes add such delightful surface realism and highlights, I use them extensively.

Fig. 5 CLOUD LAYERS. Using circular brush strokes of cloud color with ultramarine red in reflected light areas separates clouds into layers.

Fig. 6 VEGETATION. Trees painted over warmly tinted snow using the wet-on-wet method re-create the sun's highlights.

Two other handy Vintage Reproductions products are Shimmering Ice Flakes no. 815 and Sparkling Tints kit no. 720, composed of several shades of wintery blues and greens. I mix these into sheet ice, icicles, and ballast to create a frosty chill. The snows and tints are dispensed through a bellows applicator (no. 817), and forcibly puffing them creates a miniature snowstorm!

You can purchase Vintage Reproductions products at many hobby shops, through Wm. K. Walthers, or direct from 2606 Flintridge Drive, Colorado Springs, CO 80918.

Snow bases

To permanently attach snow crystals to the winterscape, I use three snow-base adhesives, depending on desired snow conditions. The first two are listed in fig. 9.

To simulate cold, dry snow, use a caulk snow base of Dow Corning Trade Mate 11 paintable white silicone. Applied with a palette knife, it forms overhanging snowbanks that don't sag or flow, and sharp wind-blown drifts that will never yellow. The paintable caulking easily accepts blue shadow tints in the final detailing.

For softer drifts of fluffy, wet snow, use the acrylic snow base. It's also used for snowy backgrounds as its soft contours enhance the illusion of distance.

Since snow has no color of its own, it reflects sky tones. A touch of acrylic phthalo blue in either snow base will draw the foreground and painted background into harmony.

For a thin layer of ground snow and for adding frost on trees, use gloss medium or hairspray as a snow base.

Plaster contours

Begin winterscape contours during the plaster phase of scenery by building up higher snowbanks around roads and tracks. Model sunlit sides of the tracks "melted" back a bit to show the radiant heat of the ballast at work.

"Grade" dirt roadways into the wet plaster. Place a sheet of plastic food wrap over the road and roll a scale vehicle back and forth until deep snow ruts appear. We'll add final details to the road later.

Form large flat fields by pouring them with soupy plaster, then use a hair dryer to blow it into natural-looking drifts.

Sift dry plaster through a tea strainer over the winterscape to provide "tooth" for the snow substrate to adhere to. To get acquainted with the snow bellows, paint a section of the plaster drifts with blue-tinted gloss medium and puff some snow into place.

River base

Puff dampened rubber rock molds with Vintage Reproductions no. 775 Granite Duster, a black glittery material that adds surface texture to the river stones, then fill the molds with plaster. Break up the castings and arrange them along the river banks to create deep pools and minor falls in the riverbed. Cement them in place with soupy plaster and at the same time build the river channel and snowbanks by scraping away the plaster run-off. Smooth out any irregularities on the water surface.

Determine the direction of the sunlight and tint the river rocks with the sunny base color, listed in fig. 10. Brush the shadow wash next, including overhangs, deep fissures, and crevices. Drybrush highlights on the sunny side of the rocks using white with a touch of yellow ochre.

Dab dormant, ochre-colored

Fig. 7 BRANCH DETAIL Use a palette knife to scratch fine branches into bare trees.

Fig. 8 SNOW MATERIALS. Winter components are being loaded for the rail ride up to the winterscape. Notice the subtle differences of snow colors and the bellows "puffer" used to create miniature snowstorms. Those pallets of icicles and layers of ice need to be quickly loaded into the safety of the awaiting refrigerator car.

lichens randomly over the rocks followed by a dark red variation to represent these tenacious coverings. Add the final dark wash to deepen shadow areas. Drybrush dark streaks on the sunlit rock faces to simulate discoloration from mineral erosion.

Scrape wave motion lines into the river with a palette knife as shown in fig. 11. Use circular swirls in the main channel and light jabs for ripples along banks and eddies.

Painting the river

Seal the river with full-strength gloss medium. Working in foot-long sections, dab in shallow water with gloss medium mixed with raw sienna and burnt and raw umber. Allow some of the plaster's white to shine through.

A touch of phthalo blue blended around the warmer rock dabs creates both individual stones and shadows as in fig 12. Paint in submerged, icy banks with white and phthalo blue, randomly grayed with a little raw umber.

Now blend a dark mix of black, phthalo blue, and raw umber into the deeper waters and streak and dot it randomly into the shallows to create small pools and wave shadows. Leave contrasting sharp and blended lines along the ice banks to simulate surface and submerged ice. Apply paint lightly —don't overpaint and spoil the depth effect of the river.

The river must dry three days before you add a topcoat of EnviroTex casting resin, so it's back to the workbench to create sparkling sheets of ice to float on the river.

Sheet ice

Modeling random sizes and shapes of sheet and skim ice is easy. Besides placing some on the river, we'll add ice over ballast as well as on structures and rolling stock.

Mix two ounces of EnviroTex with three toothpick dots of acrylic phthalo blue. From Sparkling Tints kit no. 720, add three blasts of Icy Blue and Sea Green as well as six puffs of Slushy Snow. Stir until all the particles are suspended in the resin. Haphazardly paint the ice thinly on waxed paper sheets. The, resin will bead up and re-form into hundreds of pools.

Let this cure for 20 minutes, then lightly press a clean new sheet of waxed paper over the ice and peel the two apart. You'll have two sheets of ice, each thinned down to scale thickness. Place them on a flat surface and puff Shimmering Ice Flakes over them.

As the "ice" reforms, it locks onto stray flakes to produce thin, irregular edges as shown in fig. 13.

Fig. 9 Snow Bases

Caulking snow base
3 ounces white silicone caulk
½" (from tube) white acrylic paint
Touch of acrylic phthalo blue or cadmium yellow

Acrylic snow base
1 ounce acrylic titanium white
1 ounce modeling paste
½ ounce gloss medium
½ ounce heavy gel medium
Touch of phthalo blue or cadmium yellow

Fig. 10 Winter Rock Tints

Cloudy rocks
Dissolve in 2½ ounces of water:
½" of raw umber acrylic tube paint
¼" phthalo blue
touch of red oxide

Sunny rocks
2½ ounces water
½" burnt sienna
¼" yellow ochre touch of phthalo blue

Shadow wash
2 ounces cloudy rock color
⅛" phthalo blue

Dark wash
1 ounce water
⅛" each of raw umber, phthalo blue, black

Ochre lichens
½" white
⅛" yellow ochre
touch of cadmium red and burnt sienna

Dark lichens
Divide ochre lichen mix in half and add touches of cadmium red and alizarin crimson

Fig. 11 RIVER BASE. Use a palette knife to create plaster waves and ripples in the waterway channel.

Fig. 12 RIVER SURFACE. Add shadows of blue to define individual stones in the shallow areas of the river.

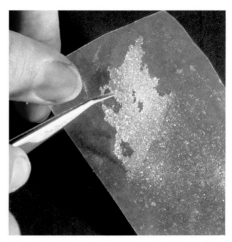

Fig. 13 SHEET ICE. Sheet ice is easily produced with EnviroTex.

To create more translucent white ice sheets, add a fine overspray of white spray paint to emulate trapped air. I intermix both types of ice on the layout to create more visual interest. After curing, the ice can easily be peeled from the waxed paper.

Finishing the river

Rainbow trout made from aluminum foil, shown in fig. 14, add an element of surprise in the river. I used Badger Air Opaque Aqua and a splash of red to color them.

Mix a batch of EnviroTex just like the ice sheets, minus the Slushy snow. Pour small amounts in the riverbed and thinly paint it into place with a disposable brush. Form deeper ⅛"-deep pools behind the falls for those hungry trout awaiting spring.

Add light spritzes of Sparkling Tints aqua and sea green around surface stones and submerged turbulence and swirl it with a toothpick. The particles will settle to the bottom, so tease them into suspension as the resin cures. They nicely animate the river with sparkling light and they also add the illusion of moving water.

Work the fiber materials from the tinting kit into the resin to create cascades and white-water rapids. My favorite is the fiber batting used

to model surface turbulence in the fast-flowing shallow areas.

Begin adding ice sheets along lingering waters and eddying pools that trap rafts of ice and broken pieces into the main channel as in fig. 15. Ice is generally found locked onto rocks and boulders, so line tip the natural holes in the ice sheets with smaller surface stones.

Lay an ice bridge completely across the channel. This bridge will later be snow-covered to mysteriously hide the river. Lightly tap the ice with a toothpick to glue it to the EnviroTex, leaving portions of trapped air showing. A light spritz of Shimmering Ice Flakes on the downriver side of the ice sheets simulates them melting.

The tinting kit includes a bellows of white foam. Add this when the EnviroTex begins to harden so that the foam remains on the top surface. Light puffs atop the fiber materials look like splashing water drops.

After the river cures, stipple and drybrush some white-water effects with white acrylic paint to further bring the river to life.

Icy ballast

Begin with 8 parts Woodland Scenics medium gray ballast mixed with light buff and black (cinders) to create highlights and shadow. Add 4 parts Vintage Reproductions

Cold-Dry Snow, and 3 parts of Sparkling Tints, using the light, medium, and dark blues. Also add 1 part Shimmering Ice Flakes and blend the materials thoroughly.

Apply the ballast and shape the roadbed, brushing it up against any snowbanks cut by engine plows. Tapping the rails with a paintbrush handle settles the ballast nicely between the ties and off the rail webs.

Use an empty bellows to puff air at a low angle down the tracks. This creates top surface veins of Sparkling Tints. Dust a final thin transparent layer of Cold Snow onto small areas and tap the rails again. Rotted crossties and a little spilled coal (denoting my railroad's main source of revenue) were the final details.

Ultra-fine misters from hairspray bottles are the best choice for prewetting ballast. They won't disturb the ballast if a first mist of denatured alcohol and a second, heavier spray of water is added. Follow this by spraying a 50/50 mix of gloss medium and water to seal the ballast. Matte medium may be added to this formula if you want a drier-looking roadbed.

Let the roadbed dry thoroughly, then begin arranging ice sheets along it. Take large pieces and drape them completely across the

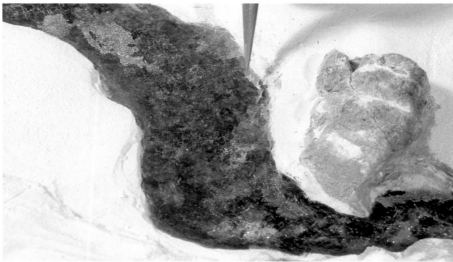

Fig. 15 FLOATING ICE. Add ice sheets along lingering waters.

Fig. 14 FOIL FISH. The game warden impatiently waits for these trout to be returned to their native waters.

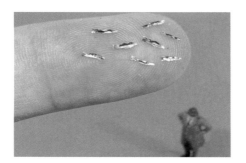

Fig. 16 ICE ALONG TRACKS. Applying the EnviroTex ice with CA "magically" simulates varying thicknesses of ice along with the cloudy appearance of trapped air.

Fig. 17 GRANULAR ICE. Create granular ice by puffing Cold-Dry Snow over hairspray.

Fig. 18 SNOW ON TRACKS. You can add snow between the rails, but don't make it any higher than the railheads.

roadbed, then cut them to fit snugly between the rails. Let other pieces lie "trapped" against ties. Small groupings that collectively resemble the remains of a snowbank appear most natural.

Work thin, curved pieces up the ballast slope from neighboring snowbanks. Leave a straight-line gap next to the sunny side of the rails, reflecting radiant heat. Apply liberal amounts of cyanoacrylate adhesive (CA) to glue the ice in place. A small piece of waxed paper between you and the sheet ice will keep fingers free of any oozing glue when pressing them down. Figure 16 shows how the CA magically fogs some areas of the ice and turns other areas crystal clear.

Wind-driven snow

Carefully mask the railheads using thin strips of tape. Spritz hairspray, then puff on some Cold-Dry Snow to create thin, granular ice as shown in fig. 17. Using the caulk snowbase, drag tiny amounts randomly down the track with a palette knife, following the natural wind direction. Snow in less windy areas should be drawn toward the heaviest flow of rail traffic.

Sweep the snow onto the ice patches to blend the areas together. Bury sections of track as shown in fig. 18, but be mindful of track clearances. A final light skim of the knife creates the look of hard-driven snow we want, particularly between the rails. Puff Cold-Dry

snow forcibly into the snowbase.

Peel the masking tape from the rails back on itself and toward the inside of the rails to clear flangeways. I made a final check of track clearances through the ice and snow using an old set of trucks with oversized flanges.

After the snow base has dried, vacuum up any stray snow. Mist the area lightly with water, then spray on a coat of the gloss medium mix to provide a protective coating. Now you can clean off the railheads and let those backed-up freights through until we grind rail traffic to a frozen halt with Part 2's blinding blizzards.

With a snowstorm sweeping over the divide, the dismayed crew pulls into the siding for a meet knowing they'll be quickly overtaken by the racing snows.

10 Modeling a winterscape: Part 2
Cold spells and melting snows

**BY RAND HOOD
PHOTOS BY RAND
AND KAREN HOOD**

In Chapter 9 we modeled a winter scene including a snow-filled forest backdrop, snowbanks, and an ice-covered river. Now we'll finish the frosty landscape, then bring on the chinook winds and thawing temperatures by modeling melting snow.

Winter vegetation

Scrawny bushes and sparse undergrowth cling for dear life through the winter months. A good product for representing these is "Wild Weeds," marketed by Timber Products (2029 E. Howe Avenue, Tempe, AZ 85281). These colored fiber battings are a perfect armature to which tiny bare branches can be applied. Mix together combinations of no. 12 Bronze and no. 15 Rust, and trim them into 1″ to 1½″ lengths. Other combinations of nos. 18, 19, and 20 (straw, barley, and wheat) are the natural blend of fall-cured grasses.

Trim them in ½″ to ¾″ lengths.

Wrap a small piece of masking tape around each bush middle and add some white glue just above the tape. When the glue dries, cut through the tape to separate each piece into two bushes. The result is head-high willow brush and scrubby grass clumps. Stick them in ⅛″ holes on a 12″-long 1 x 4, as shown in fig. 1.

Add lacy branches to the willows by first spraying them with a slow-drying satin clear varnish spray. Puff Vintage Reproduction's long flocking fibers on the armature

Fig. 1 BUSHES. Blended bushes are about to receive winter colors.

Fig. 2 TREES. Use a palette knife to sweep acrylic snow base on pine trees.

Fig. 3 SNOWBASE. Use a palette knife to add the snow base. Doing this is quite similar to frosting a cake.

Fig. 4 PLANTING VEGETATION. Only the tallest of bushes poke through heavy snow. Note how deep snowbanks have engulfed parts of the river.

Fig. 5 WEEDS. Press Woodland Scenics field grass into the wet snow base until the base grabs hold of the grass fibers.

Fig. 6 FOOTPRINTS. Judging by the number of footprints through the snow, the game warden has thoroughly checked the area.

with the firm's plastic bellows. Use no. 809 Brown followed by more spray and shorter fibers of no. 795 Russet and cool lavender and blues from kit nos. 717 and 718.

Finish the grass clumps by adding long fibers of no. 810 Gold. After the clumps dry, cut just above the tape so the bottom spreads out into individual branches. When planted in the snow base they give the illusion of snow-wallowed bushes.

To "cool" pine trees, spray them with varnish and puff them with some Vintage Reproductions nos. 803 Olive Green and 804 Blue-Green pine needles. When they dry, "winterize" them with a few downward swipes of acrylic snow base, using the palette knife as in fig. 2, then puff them liberally with snow. (Snow base formulas were listed in part 1.)

Bare trees also receive a light

Fig. 7 Winter Scenery Mixes

Damp earth wash
- ½ ounce gloss medium
- ½ ounce water
- 1¼" raw umber tube acrylic
- ¼" phthalo blue tube acrylic
- ¼" black tube acrylic

Sleet mix
- 2 ounces gloss medium
- 1 ounce heavy gel medium
- ⅛" white tube acrylic toothpick dot of phthalo blue
- 2 tablespoons of Slushy snow
- 2 tablespoons of Cold-Dry snow

Glaze mix
Divide sleet mix in half and add:
- ½ ounce gloss medium
- 1 teaspoon Slushy snow

Fig. 8 SNOW HIGHLIGHTS. Use a wide brush to add the acrylic snow base on various surfaces.

coating of snow. While you're at it, add snow to the tops of lineside details such as telephone poles and signals.

Spreading the snow base

Rewet the raw plaster scenery base. Use a palette knife to spread a ⅛" layer of acrylic snow base over an 18"-square area as in fig. 3. Giving the area periodic mists of water will keep the surface workable for 20 minutes. Lightly skip the knife across the surface in one direction to establish windflow. Use sideward sweeps of the knife to spread snow up to rock faces and other snowtrapping obstacles.

On the icy side of knolls, whip up cresting snowbanks with the knife tip and taper them back to the rippled snow. Bury sections of the river, leaving a thin edge of ice showing, and cap river rocks and trapped ice with snow.

Dragging the knife over rocky outcroppings leaves snow edges projecting into space. The key to realism is to be loose and let the snowdrifts form naturally.

Using the knife edge, whirl the snow base along the ballast and up the slope to create icy fingers that unite the roadbed and winterscape. Sprinkle patches of rocky soil on wind-swept embankments and open fields. Press these in and then cap talus rock and clumps of yellow ground foam with snow. Sink in mailboxes, barrels, or animals for extra detail.

Now stand back and let those snow bellows wail. Puff some Blue Slushy snow in the shadows and under the overhangs for extra depth. Blast away with white snow everywhere—let those snowflakes fly!

Adding vegetation

One big advantage of modeling winter scenery is that you can add snow and plant vegetation simultaneously. Simply dip the end of each bush in a container of snow base and apply it anywhere into the surface snow base. Dab the bush onto the snow until it sinks in and grabs hold.

Plant bushes in groups and have them overhanging the river, but away from hidden shallows, as in fig. 4. Puff extra snow on any exposed snow base around bushes to create trapped snow in the lower branches. The loose piles will be glued down later.

Cut Woodland Scenics harvest gold field grass to ³⁄₁₆" lengths and apply them loosely. Hold the material between your fingers, move the grass up and down until the snow base catches the fibers, then lightly pull straight up as fig. 5 shows.

Add heavily concentrated growth, then feather out the edges until they disappear into the winterscape. Don't worry if the grasses seem a little tall—you can trim them lower when everything dries completely.

Add tiny footprints of scavenging animals with a toothpick. Carve extra shoe detail on the bottom of a one-legged figure and take him for a walk through the woods. Dragging the heel before pressing down creates the human stride, as shown in fig. 6.

Not all the snow powder you apply will stick once the snow base dries. Mist "wet" water (water with a bit of dish detergent added) over everything, including vegetation and rock faces, followed by a mist of diluted gloss medium to seal these materials in place.

Add light puffs of Slushy Snow into the shadow side of rocks. When the final coat dries, randomly trim some of the winter grasses with scissors, then vacuum the area.

Dot a touch of phthalo blue mixed with gloss medium into the footprints to highlight them. Brush

29

Fig. 9. RECEDING SNOW. Soggy snow-banks shed their water in glistening run-off. Note the wet snow at the base of the cliff and the damp soil surrounding it.

Fig. 10 FROSTY TIES. Apply a mask so that the shadow-protected area is exposed. White paint, snow base, and puffed snow leave a frosty appearance on the ties.

some of this mix under the tree-shadowed forest floor, but be subtle.

Using white glue, fix trees and lineside details into predrilled holes. Spritz snow to cover any oozing glue.

Transitional areas

Transitional snow areas are needed to feather the heavy accumulations of snow back to scenicked "dry" landscape. (If you are changing seasons, substitute greens with yellow ground foam.) Lighter snows along the storm edge melt rapidly from the earth's radiant heat. Meanwhile, older and heavier interior snows collect, overpowering the scene with white.

I based this transition scene on the rainy landscape described in Chapter 7, "Modeling a 'Rainscape.'" Mask the rails and saturate the entire area, including ballast and track, with the damp earth wash listed in fig. 7. Brush rainlike streaks down rocks and cuts

and darken areas where water naturally collects, then gently fade the wash into the "dry" scenery.

Let that dry 30 minutes, then change directions and begin adding withering streaks of the glaze mix, following the prevailing winds. Gradually increase the accumulation with heavier strokes until the glaze meets the solidly covered snow area.

Now add the sleet mix following the same procedure, but begin about 4″ shy of the glaze edge. Also add sleet to tree fronts facing the wind. Realistic patterns emerge as the ground cover snags the snow. Cuts, ditches, and inner rail curves are also natural snow traps and receive a heavier brushing of sleet.

Add final detailing using the acrylic snowbase. Sweep it lightly across the tracks and add heavy accumulations on windstruck slopes as shown in fig. 8. Tighten the brushstrokes until you have an

unbroken coating and blend it over existing solid snow. Add additional wind-blown patterns using the palette knife, and add fine tendrils of snow with a small brush.

Starting at the glazy forefront, puff Slushy Snow, then change to Fluffy-Wet and finally Cold-Dry snows before meeting the solid snow. Turning a full bellows upside-down and lightly squeezing produces a thin trickle of snow that helps to draw more attention against wind obstacles. Seal the loose snow with a mist of water followed by diluted gloss medium.

Sun 'n' snow

Figure 9 shows how sun and rising temperatures create soggy snowbanks as the last strongholds of snow recede. Add a touch more phthalo blue into the acrylic snow base to reflect the atmosphere of cloudless skies.

With palette knife in hand, imagine where snow was once piled high and draw in the thin, smooth-edged remains of snowbanks. Leave small traces with a toothpick. Add snow under shadowy outcroppings and crevices to represent the last cool gasp of dying snow. Press a few ice sheets over larger snowpacks to create areas of crusty snow. Then add a sparse brushing of the glaze and sleet mix over the ice and against the shaded side of plants.

Puff Slushy Snow on the downhill side of the patches, then apply FluffyWet onto exposed snowbases. A light mist of water on the surface of sunny patches softens them so that they appear to be melting. Plant winter bushes warmed with a little no. 794 Medium Golden Brown in deeper snowbanks.

We still need some visual evidence of melting. You can create the appearance of wet soil on the downslope side of patches with a wash of 50/50 Scalecoat clear gloss and Minwax Dark Walnut stain. Streak it down rockfaces for trickling run-off. Work away from snowfaces and allow the stain to be drawn under the snow. Areas where overflow collects receive a deeper wash of uncut stain. Add ribbons of water feeding overburdened streams to complete the run-off cycle. When everything is dry, recoat the stains with gloss to bring on a wet sheen.

Frosty cool

Set up a light source to throw shadows onto the landscape, then use cyanoacrylate adhesive (CA) to glue ice sheets in the shadows. Overhang a few of these from the rocks to simulate sliding ice. Use brushed sleet mix to accentuate the shadow line and work inward with acrylic snowbase, dragging crests onto ice sheets and against vegetation. Add puffs of Slushy and Cold-Dry snow.

Give open areas the sun and snow treatment of melting snows and watery run-off. A mist of diluted gloss medium into the

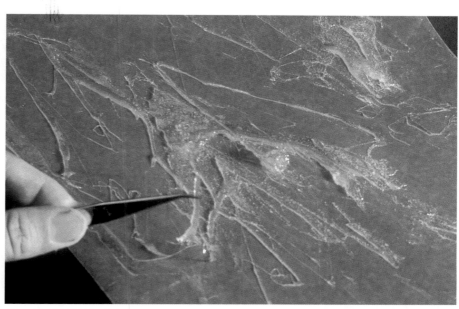

Fig. 11 MAKING ICICLES. A large portion of the icicles will be unusable, but there are enough delicate forms for a small scene.

Fig. 12 ADDING ICICLES. The melting snow has created lots of icicles above the portal at tunnel no. 3.

shadows followed by a fine spritz of Shimmering Ice Flakes and Cold-Dry snow from the bellows completes the frosty atmosphere.

Frost-covered ties

Ballast stores heat, rapidly melting frost and snow, but ice remains on ties because wood is a natural insulator. The technique in fig. 10 can be used for either tie covering.

Outline tree or rock shadows on ballast with masking tape. Also

mask the rails and scenicked area to protect it from overspray. Add a thin strip of tape to simulate where the reflected warmth of the rail has already begun melting the cold coverings. For frosty ties, lightly mist them with white spray paint, feathering it out at the outer reaches of the shadow.

Snowy ties receive a light brushing of the acrylic snow base followed by puffs of Shimmering Ice Flakes and Cold-Dry snow. Spritz

Fig. 13 RUTTED ROAD. The maintenance truck is skidding a little as the driver negotiates the deep snow ruts.

Fig. 14 MELTING SNOW ON ROAD. When the snow melts, the rancher's road will be a quagmire.

frosty ties with hairspray and puff them with the same ice and snow. Peel off the mask and let this dry completely.

Add "Cold Ballast" (from part 1) between the ties and tap the rails to settle it. Blend in regular ballast near the frosty edges and down the sunny roadbed as shown in fig. 10. Mist the ballast with denatured alcohol and apply diluted gloss medium in the frosty areas and matte medium in the sunny locations. When this dries, add a light brushing of the sleet mix into any shadowy recesses.

Icicles

The freeze-and-thaw cycles of frosty cool weather form cascading ice in downward run-off as well as plenty of icicles from dripping snowmelt. To create icicles, mix a batch of the Sheet Ice formula from part 1, but leave it in its mixing container about 30 minutes until it reaches a taffy-like consistency.

Turn the container upside down onto a sheet of waxed paper, then drag and stretch out strands of the resin. Tiny icicles will appear among the larger "cascading" ice

as in fig. 11. Cut the ice, then use CA to glue the pieces in concentrated areas, matching criss-crossing icicles to rock ledges and crevices as shown in fig. 12.

Road conditions

The snow-rutted road created last month is still covered only with plaster. Rewet it and brush on blue-tinted gloss medium. Lightly puff the road with snow and smooth the surface using clear plastic food wrap. Let it dry.

Use the frozen ballast mix from part 1 and add 1 part dirt. Apply this to the ruts only, then mist it with water and diluted gloss medium. Add a couple of random puffs of wind-blown snow into the ruts.

Make plowed snow along the road with a mixture of ground-up white beaded Styrofoam and acrylic snow base. Work plain snow base around and over the pile to blend and create overhanging crests. Puff Slushy Snow in the shadows and either Fluffy or Cold Snow over the rest. You can see the completed road in fig. 13.

Create melting snows on roads by masking thin tire tracks through

shadows and blown drifts. Add a few ice sheets between the tire tracks, then use the palette knife to sculpt acrylic snow base patches. Pull the masking tape back on itself and puff the road with Slushy and Fluffy Snow. Draw muddy runoff using glossy stain and dab where the snows have already melted as fig. 14 shows.

Snowy trains

My helper units assigned to the tunnel district were natural candidates for snow applied to locomotive plows and walkways. Use the caulking snowbase applied with a toothpick and fine brush as fig. 15 shows. The snow easily peels off when dry, so I became a little more daring in applying it.

Puff Cold-Dry Snow onto the snow base. Don't let stray flakes get near any gears. There will be tiny fibers that upon closer examination look unrealistic—press them back along the edges to settle them into the snow base.

There's nothing like snow-covered rolling stock to animate the winterscape. I went into my railroad scrapyard, found some willing subjects, and "winter sal-

Fig. 15 SNOW ON PLOWS. The caulking snow base can be easily removed from locomotives if your layout experiences a sudden heat wave.

Fig. 16 CAR ROOF. Practice snow techniques on an old car before adding snow to a prized model.

Fig. 17 COAL LOAD. Use a combination of sheet ice and snow base to winterize coal loads.

Fig. 18 MELTING CARS. Stain and thinner create the melted run-off; ice sheets and caulking complete the effect of melting snow.

vaged" them—now they're among my favorite cars.

Use the caulking snow base on revenue cars. Skim boxcar roofs with a palette knife to let a few ribs show through, and coat them where wheels kick up snow. With a toothbrush and a dot of Badger Air Opaque White, splatter snow upward as in fig. 16.

I gave removable coal hopper loads a few ice sheets and skimmed them with the snow base directionally against the coal as in fig. 17.

Snow on cars descending from the storms quickly melts. In order for wet streaks to appear, they must be darker than the car's main color. The 1:1 mix of Scalecoat gloss and Minwax Dark Walnut stain works nicely for common red and brown cars.

Brush on puddles and run-off, and allow capillary action to draw it along rib seams. Random touches of thinner spread the stain so it looks like partially evaporated water. Allow the stain to dry, then add more gloss to bring out a wet sheen as fig. 18 shows.

Use CA to glue ice sheets under running boards and against roof ribs in a few thin ribbons. Apply caulking and puff on Slushy and Wet Snow. Realign stray snow fibers, then add a few footprints on the running boards accentuated with a blue tint.

Fig. 19 WINTRY ROOF. Sheet ice around the chimney, along with plenty of firewood, show that the cabin's occupant is keeping a fire blazing.

Covering rooftops with the melting snow is also effective. Figure 19 shows a lonely mountain cabin swept by a previous storm. Note the icy freeze/thaw effect around the chimney.

Winter lighting

Single fluorescent lighting fixtures with cool white tubes enhance the chilly nature of the winterscape. Position the fixtures around the layout so that they cast light in the sharp southern angle of the winter sun.

Photographic color gels can be cut to fit inside the plastic diffuser covering to further cool and weaken the light source. Roscolux gels, available at camera stores, have a wide range of colors and transparencies. To create a nice daylight effect, no. 53 Pale Lavender with a transparency of 64 percent fills the shadows with color. For a moody nighttime atmosphere, I use separate (and fewer) fluorescents and no. 378 Alice Blue gels with a 15 percent transparency.

Additional dimmable incandescent lighting will create sunny highlights on the daytime snow. Dimming these lights provides soft general illumination for night operations.

Well, we've covered a lot of ground (literally!), and I hope the aura of winter will shine through on your layout.

Trees

11 Trees, trees, and more trees

Eight simple ways to make trees from common materials

Model trees can be made in dozens of ways. These HO scale trees were made using string, wire, ground foam, dowels, twigs, and other common materials.

BY ART CURREN
PHOTOS BY THE AUTHOR

Our first impression of a layout as we enter a train room is usually the scenery we see, and often a major part of that scenery is trees. To get model trees, we can buy 'em, find 'em, or make 'em, and although we certainly can't be expected to make trees branch by branch and leaf by leaf, we can get pretty close to natural-looking trees with many modeling methods. This overview provides a look at several methods, most of which can be used in any scale.

Basic tree shapes

Model trees generally have two parts: the trunk/branch structure and the foliage material. Most commercial and scratchbuilt model trees follow the same basic form. The trunk (flexible plastic or metal) is bent so the branches radiate outward, then it's painted. Next, a fibrous material representing the smaller branches is glued to the larger branches. Colored ground foam is then added to represent leaves.

Fig. 1. IMPROVING READY-MADE TREES. The stock Life-Like tree at left needs some help. Spray-painting the tree gray and adding ground foam over the wet paint greatly improved the appearance of the two trees at right.

Fig. 2. WEED TREES. Some weeds can be used as trees by spray-painting them green; others can be used by combining them and adding ground foam.

Fig. 4. BOTTLE-BRUSH TREES. Many types of trees can be created using the bottle-brush method.

Campbell and Color Rite make evergreen trees using tapered trunks. Holes are drilled around the trunk's circumference, into which small pieces of air fern are inserted to make the boughs. Sometimes ground foam can be added to these boughs for a different look. These trees require some work, since it takes a while to insert each individual branch.

Enhancing ready-made trees

Since ready-made trees are mass-produced, they can't be painstakingly handcrafted in every detail. Thus, they often need a little additional work. Many have a large base cast onto the bottom of the trunk, enabling them to stand on a flat tabletop. I usually cut this off with side-cutting pliers.

Some premade trees have too much ground foam on them, hiding the branch structure and making them appear too solid. Removing some foam with tweezers will open up the tree.

If you look outside, you'll see many shades of gray tree trunks and very few brown ones. Painting trunks with Floquil 110012 Reefer Gray or 110013 Grimy Black enhances their appearance.

Other trees may require more help such as adding new cover or altering the colors or shape. Figure 1 shows an example. For tree cover I generally use Woodland Scenics coarse and fine grades of foam.

Making a more ragged profile on commercial evergreens by cutting out a few branch ends and adding foam or flocking makes them more realistic. I prefer flocking on evergreens, since it better resembles the needles.

Trees that are too bright can be toned down with a wash of India ink or Rit fabric dye (Kelly Green) applied with a pump spray bottle. I use a mix of about 15 parts isopropyl (rubbing) alcohol to 1 part India ink, and I dilute the Rit dye

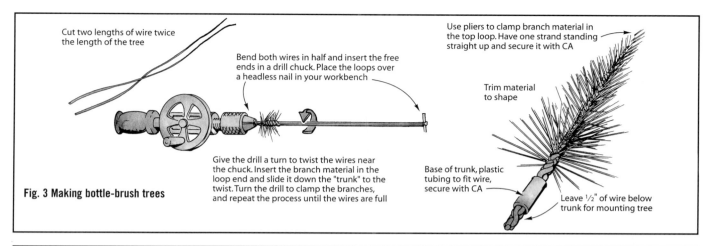

Cut two lengths of wire twice the length of the tree

Bend both wires in half and insert the free ends in a drill chuck. Place the loops over a headless nail in your workbench

Give the drill a turn to twist the wires near the chuck. Insert the branch material in the loop end and slide it down the "trunk" to the twist. Turn the drill to clamp the branches, and repeat the process until the wires are full

Use pliers to clamp branch material in the top loop. Have one strand standing straight up and secure it with CA

Trim material to shape

Base of trunk, plastic tubing to fit wire, secure with CA

Leave 1/2" of wire below trunk for mounting tree

Fig. 3 Making bottle-brush trees

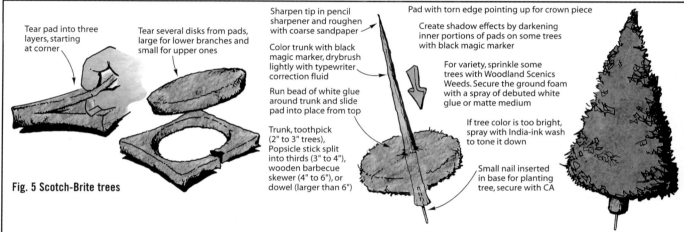

Tear pad into three layers, starting at corner

Tear several disks from pads, large for lower branches and small for upper ones

Sharpen tip in pencil sharpener and roughen with coarse sandpaper

Color trunk with black magic marker, drybrush lightly with typewriter correction fluid

Run bead of white glue around trunk and slide pad into place from top

Trunk, toothpick (2" to 3" trees), Popsicle stick split into thirds (3" to 4"), wooden barbecue skewer (4" to 6"), or dowel (larger than 6")

Pad with torn edge pointing up for crown piece

Create shadow effects by darkening inner portions of pads on some trees with black magic marker

For variety, sprinkle some trees with Woodland Scenics Weeds. Secure the ground foam with a spray of debuted white glue or matte medium

If tree color is too bright, spray with India-ink wash to tone it down

Small nail inserted in base for planting tree, secure with CA

Fig. 5 Scotch-Brite trees

to half the strength recommended on the package.

Simulating sunlight hitting the tops and outermost edges of the leaves can be done by spraying a mist of light-colored paint from a distance of about 24″. Spray from the top only, using yellow for deciduous trees and blue/gray or gray for evergreens. I use various brands of inexpensive spray paints found in hardware stores.

Homemade trees

Why make your own trees when there are so many ready-made and kit trees available on the market? One obvious reason is the cost. Another reason is that you'll need more trees than you ever dreamed you would, and you can get a greater variety of sizes and shapes by making them yourself. Most of the materials needed to scratch-build trees can be found in craft,

flower, hardware, and grocery stores as well as hobby shops.

Photos of real trees show how asymmetrical most are. I try to model tree profiles rather than the actual bough structure. Another key to a good-looking tree is the openness of its silhouette. Against a sky this is obvious. However, if there's another tree behind the one you're looking at, it seems more dense because the background tree is filling in behind, eliminating the see-through effect. Keep this in mind by using open trees when placing trees against a sky backdrop.

Weed trees

One of the oldest methods is to use weeds for trees. This method is certainly economical. Try to find weeds that duplicate trees in miniature. Autumn is the best time of the year to gather weeds.

When I find weeds that look like

trees, I simply spray-paint them green after a little trimming with a small scissors. I hit the tops with a spray of yellow, as mentioned earlier, and I have a tree! If weeds have the right shape to use as an armature but the flowers or seed pods aren't good enough to use as-is, I spray them gray and add green ground foam. Figure 2 shows a few examples.

One drawback of weeds is that they're very fragile. I add lengths of music wire up into the hollow stems to provide strength. Painting helps hold the flowers or seed pods together. Weeds also have thin stems, sometimes too thin to represent a decent trunk. To fix this I wrap string or thread around the bottom part of the stem to thicken it. I bond this with cyanoacrylate adhesive (CA), then paint all exposed branches and the trunk dark gray or black.

Fig. 6. ROOT-PROTECTOR TREES. Pull the white filter off and cut the cushion into smaller pieces. Place a large piece over the dowel point and push it down with the wires still pointing up through the cushion. Repeat, alternating big and small pieces on up the trunk and even above the dowel. Secure the cushions by twisting the ends of the wires together. You can leave the ends of the wires sticking up or push them down into the cushion. Ground foam adds texture.

Fig. 7. STRING-SACK TREES. Begin by inserting at least six lengths of wire through a wood dowel. Bend the ends of the wire upward. Cover this frame with rectangles of the string-sack material and paint the whole assembly gray. Spray with a fixative and apply coarse ground foam.

Weeds are often lopsided, with their branches all heading one way. Some of these can be used in corners of a layout where this isn't noticeable. By joining two of these lopsided weeds together with a wrapping of thread, a presentable tree can be achieved.

Bottle-brush trees

Another ancient yet still useful treemaking method is the bottle-brush technique. Wires are twisted around strands of string or fibers, thereby capturing them inside the "trunk." Most modelers think of this method only for making evergreens, but it can also be used for deciduous trees.

You'll need a hand drill to use this technique, as shown in fig. 3. The wires near the chuck end of the drill will twist first.

You can use lengths of string, twine, or other fibers as branches. The type of fiber you use determines what kind of tree will result. I use green rug yarn, green cord, or white cotton string dyed green with Rit dye for the evergreens, and synthetic twine or three-stranded cotton cord for the deciduous trees.

Leave some room between the lowest branch and the chuck so this part of the twisted wires can become the trunk. Be careful not to twist too tightly, or the tension will snap the wires. The wire will twist tightest at the chuck end. Trim evergreens with a taper toward the top, as fig. 4 shows. Then brush the cotton string with a steel-bristled brush to bring out the minute fibers.

The three-stranded cord for the deciduous trees is divided into three separate segments about one-third of the way from the outer ends. Apply CA to these branches to stiffen them, then spray the tree gray or black.

When using synthetic twine, be sure to trim it and pull each segment apart until small individual branches radiate from the wire trunk. Use black or dark gray for coloring. I sometimes use synthetic twine for evergreens, trimming it to a taper, spraying it black, and adding green flocking or fine dark green ground foam.

Spray unflocked evergreens with clear finish to stiffen the branches.

The deciduous trees will get a covering of green ground foam.

Scotch-Brite trees

Building these trees, as fig. 5 shows, is a matter of tearing a series of disks from a green Scotch-Brite scouring pad and pushing them over a trunk. Don't cut the pads, because tearing provides the ragged edges we need.

On tall trees where the lower branches begin farther up the trunk, I add stubs of fallen branches just below the first branch. I drill holes through the trunk 90 degrees from each other and insert short pieces of paper clips through the holes so they protrude from both sides. I then blacken them and add tiny scraps of pad to the ends of some of the stubs. You can see these in the lead photo.

Scotch-Brite evergreens can be made to look like dead trees by assembling them with the thin pieces of pad, painting the tree a light gray, and adding a mist of Pactra no. 1123 Light Earth or Testor's no. 1942 Dark Tan.

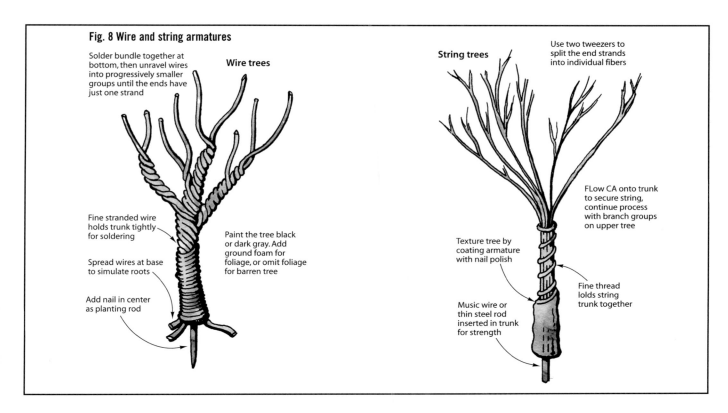

Fig. 8 Wire and string armatures

Wire trees

Solder bundle together at bottom, then unravel wires into progressively smaller groups until the ends have just one strand

Fine stranded wire holds trunk tightly for soldering

Spread wires at base to simulate roots

Add nail in center as planting rod

Paint the tree black or dark gray. Add ground foam for foliage, or omit foliage for barren tree

String trees

Use two tweezers to split the end strands into individual fibers

FLow CA onto trunk to secure string, continue process with branch groups on upper tree

Texture tree by coating armature with nail polish

Fine thread lolds string trunk together

Music wire or thin steel rod inserted in trunk for strength

Furnace (and other) filters can be used to make trees in the same manner. I use both the green fiberglass type and the black polyester kind. Assemble the trees and cover them with ground foam. They'll be more dense, so make sure they have a ragged profile.

Root-protector trees

Head for the plant store and get some Jobe's Root Protector Cushions. These consist of woven plastic material that's about ½" thick.

Begin by making a dowel trunk, finishing it as before. Drill two holes in the lower part of the trunk and insert a piece of wire in each. Figure 6 shows how to finish the armature.

Spray the tree with clear finish and add ground foam. I used Woodland Scenics Blended Turf for leaves, since it has both light- and dark-green material. If any of the wire shows below the lower part of the branches, thicken it with nail polish and paint it to match the trunk. If you want a forked trunk, use a forked twig instead of a dowel. Drill holes for

the wires in each fork top and proceed as before.

String-sack trees

This method requires a woven-string sack of the kind that holds produce; the string type works better than the plastic. The tree is made somewhat like an umbrella. Figure 7 shows the construction steps. I use nail polish to thicken the wires where they meet the trunk.

Use thread and CA to hold the material in place. The wire ends can also be bent around the string. Once you've formed the shell, cut out a few strands of string to create some holes larger than the sack weave. Stagger these and don't cut near any of the branch ends. Be sure to apply ground foam to the inside of the shell as well as the outside.

If the holes in the mesh begin to plug up, defeating the see-through look, wait until everything has dried and remove the foam from some openings with small tweezers. This makes an open tree with a very uniform profile.

There's a fabric called "tulle" or "netting" found in fabric stores

that can be used in the same manner. Since it has smaller openings, it works well on small frames with fine foam representing the leaves.

Wire armatures

For making wire armatures you'll need some heavy-gauge stranded copper electrical wire, woven steel cable, or plastic-covered steel clothesline.

As fig. 8 shows, the wire armatures are formed by grouping wires together at the base to form a trunk and soldering them together. The wires are then unraveled into progressively smaller groups until the ends have only one strand of wire. Paint the trunk and add foliage as with other armatures.

Woodland Scenics' foliage clusters work well on wire (and similar) armatures. This material appears to be coarse ground foam bonded together in clumps. Add some Walthers Goo to the end of a wire, and push on a cluster to represent leaves. Though the clusters are dense, the tree itself isn't dense because the clusters are separated. Figure 9 shows some examples.

Fig. 9. WIRE TREES. You can create just about any tree shape you heed by using wire armatures.

String trees

This technique is similar to the wire method, but substitutes string for wire. It eliminates the bloody fingers you sometimes get working with the sharp-ended wire. The end branches of the string are very fine and realistically capture the lacy look of an elaborate branch structure.

I like to use carpet thread; other kinds of string and twine will provide different characteristics. Figure 8 shows how to build a string tree. Many types of leafless trees can be made using this method, including forked or multiple-trunked trees. You can see a couple of examples in the lead photo.

Beautifully modeled tree-filled hillsides have been shown many times in magazines, but there's hardly ever a dead tree among them. Nothing makes a living tree seem more alive than the contrast of a few dead ones alongside. If any string tree doesn't live up to my standards, I just use it as another armature to be covered with ground foam.

If I know I'm making a tree with leaves, I generally use macrame yarn, a woven yarn much like clothesline rope. I bond it around a wire and separate individual strands. These strands easily spread into their individual fibers as they're unraveled, so thread is needed to wrap the larger branches back together again. CA will stiffen and bond these where they join the main trunk. Fluff out the end fibers, paint, and add ground foam as before. Synthetic twine produces straight branches. Cotton string will produce twisted branches with lots of small fibers sticking out everywhere.

Stumps and root trees

Nothing beats real tree twigs for making realistic tree stumps. Twigs even have concentric growth rings in miniature. As the lead photo shows, I used a razor saw to cut a few stumps using the lumberjack method of alternating side cuts, one slightly above the other. I snapped off other stumps to represent trees felled by natural causes. Adding a felled tree next to its stump makes a nice scene. Twigs can also serve as tree armatures—treat them like other armatures once you've trimmed and painted them.

To make a root system for a stump, drill a small hole into the flat bottom and insert a pin. Cut a piece of plastic sandwich bag, place it on a soft surface, and pin the stump through the plastic to the surface. Next run a bead of plastic wood filler around the stump base. Using a jumbo paper clip as a tool, push the filler toward the stump. The round end of the paper clip blends the roots into the trunk and separates the filler into rootlike tentacles. Flow on CA to bond everything, and let it sit overnight. You can add roots to any tree this way, especially those with dowel trunks.

After painting my stumps dark gray, I textured them with typewriter correction fluid or flat white paint. To do this, brush the stump (or tree trunk) with an almost-dry brush. This will lightly streak the stumps.

Many of the weeds mentioned earlier can do double duty since their roots make good-looking dead trees. Wash off the dirt, trim extra-long roots, and paint them gray.

Other tree and leaf materials

Lichen is a scenery staple. It's best suited for small bushes, but when covered with foam it makes an acceptable underlayment on twig trunks.

Bumpy chenille is another material that can be used for smaller evergreens. It needs to be toned down in color intensity with paint or an India-ink wash. It can also be covered with foam.

Final details

If you want a leaf-like ground cover beneath your forest, raid a pencil sharpener and spread its contents under the trees as dead leaves. Highball Products' no. 161 light green grass (dyed sawdust) makes an ideal material to dust over a darker colored tree to create sunlight highlights.

Why not have a few recently broken branches on an otherwise healthy tree? Just make a miniature tree with the same material used on the live portion and paint it tan and gray, then add it to the live tree.

A trunk can be textured to look more like bark by scraping a saw blade up and down it prior to painting. Highlight the trunk with correction fluid and flow on a wash of the India ink to further enhance it.

Now when you need trees, you'll be able to buy 'em, find 'em, and make 'em. If your layout is like most, you'll always need more trees.

12 Building forests on the M&K Division

A fast and easy way to make tree-covered mountains

BY DON CASSLER
PHOTOS BY THE AUTHOR

The M&K Division is located deep in the mountains of West Virginia. The Allegheny Mountains in this region consist of long, high ridges that are heavily forested. They are too steep for farming, so they have not been cleared.

To make our HO version of the M&K look "at home," my friends and I have had to construct plaster mountains on the layout and cover them with dense forests like those that cover the real mountains in West Virginia.

The work hasn't been difficult, and the results have been very rewarding. If you are building a similar layout and want to include heavily forested mountains, the concepts and techniques that we've developed may be of interest.

The real mountains

Our informal group has made several trips to West Virginia. These field trips have given us opportunities to study the terrain and the Baltimore & Ohio lines that our layout is based on. They have also helped us catch the essence of the region in our modeling efforts, particularly the heavily forested mountains.

Figure 1 is a good example of the terrain we're trying to duplicate. When you look at a mountain in the near distance, several important impressions register. First, trees lose their individual identity, with their varied colors blending together. Second, the hillsides assume a uniform yet roughly text appearance in a color that's peculiar to the flora of the region.

Another notable impression is that the hillsides, when viewed

Fig. 1. The mountaintop along the skyline is a good representation of what can be modeled on a forest mountain layout. Contrast the skyline with the foreground trees trackside. Also notice the varied colors in the foreground grasses and trees, as opposed to the uniform background color.

directly, appear much steeper than they actually are. Old worn-down mountains like the Alleghenies generally assume an angle of 3 feet horizontal for 1 foot of vertical rise. When looking at these hills directly, however, they appear to be so steep that you would have great difficulty climbing them.

The model mountain

Texture, color, and slope are the three most important aspects to consider when modeling forested mountains. All three work strongly to our advantage, and we use them when duplicating mountainous

terrain for our model railroads.

Of the three, I believe the most important is the apparent steepness of hills. Most mountains on our layouts are viewed directly, which means we can construct hills that are almost vertical, yet still appear to be correct and plausible. Not even the largest club has enough space to construct scale-size, properly sloped mountains.

The selective compression practiced in building mountains is the greatest jump from reality that any of us make, yet it doesn't appear unrealistic. That's probably because we don't actually "see" the

Fig. 2. This photo illustrates several of the ideas in this article. Note the steepness of the mountain, which appears natural in the area with trees. This is a transition mix of lichen and poly fiber forest. The lichen has not yet been sprinkled with foam for a color match. In the foreground is a row of tapered toothpicks for placing trees on the mountain.

mountains when we look at a model railroad. Rather, we "see" the tracks, trains, and structures. Our mind's eye registers the mountains as a background, and if we do our work well enough to re-create the impressions just described, our minds will make the scene look right.

Because our mind pushes the mountains away, it's important to avoid placing anything on them that brings them back into the foreground. This includes structures, poles, tanks, or anything else that your mind will relate to their scale size. Save such gems of detail for the foreground, where they can be seen and appreciated. I try to avoid placing anything of such nature above the highest track level.

There are exceptions to all of these generalizations, of course.

My advice is to temporarily place a structure or two in the area where you plan to violate the rule and look at it critically for a few days before you take any irrevocable steps. The question to ask yourself is whether the scene is part of the foreground or the background. If it's in the background, don't place any attention-getters there.

With these concepts in mind, let's get started building a forest.

Trees and forests

It's necessary to differentiate between building trees and building forests. In the foreground, where there are size-related structures, I build detailed trees, mostly from Woodland Scenics. I use the larger sizes here because they are more in scale with the surrounding details. Look around outside, and you'll see that many trees are taller

than the surrounding houses. I don't use too many of these trees, but the effect of size can be established by using only a few. Most of these big trees are located between the viewer and the track.

Behind the tracks, where the mountains begin, I use a slightly different technique. The beginning of the forest needs tree detail because it's really a part of the foreground. We see these trees "up close" when we look at the tracks, cars, and foreground scenery. To accomplish this effect, I plant a row of smaller Woodland Scenic trees parallel to the tracks and about an inch or two beyond the required clearance for trains. I also plant bushes around the foot of this row of trees and taper it down toward the ground. This understory fills in a glaring gap in the scenery.

Fig. 3. The row of detailed trees and forest understory tapering toward the track can be seen in this photo. The mixed poly fiber and lichen behind the trees has no limb structure.

Once again, it's helpful to carefully observe the way Mother Nature does it.

Immediately behind this row of foreground trees, I stop building trees and start building a forest. Here I abandon all detail work on trees and shift to trying to duplicate a distant forest. This work is easy and quick.

I use Bachmann Poly Fibre balls covered with Woodland Scenics Coarse Turf ground foam. These covered "trees" are glued directly to the stained plaster mountain with no space between them. This forest covers the mountain entirely. A typical example of this construction in progress is shown in fig. 2.

Coloring plaster

It's a waste of time and money to texture areas that you're going to forest. You can't see any of them when the forest is in place. For this reason, I extend the dry coloring and texturing only an inch or so into the forest border of trees and foliage and around rock outcrops or other geological features where detailed scenery will be constructed.

The important step in preparation for building a forest is to stain the plaster a deep gray so that white plaster spots don't show through. The colors of a distant mountain consist of a subdued green foliage and black shadows. That's all. The dark stained plaster provides the dark texturing of shadows. No other preliminary coloring is required. To get this deeper color, I use black Rit dye, but diluted only about half as much as the dye I use for foreground work.

As your forest building progresses, you'll notice that model forests soak up light. What appeared to be brilliant lighting before will seem quite dim until you get used to it.

Making foreground trees

The instructions included in tree kits adequately explain the procedure. All I would add is that my best results are achieved when using several small pieces of foliage material instead of one large piece. I stretch that material so it isn't dense and frequently go back after the trees are in place and stretch it out even more.

Occasionally there is a hole where I add a few more pieces of stretched foliage to make things look better. This is best done after all the surrounding foliage is in place.

I glue trees and ground cover foliage in place with silicon glue.

Foliage color

I have adopted a uniform system of colors for all the foliage on my layout. It's based on the standard colors offered by Woodland Scenics. Such a system can be built around any manufacturer's materials, but it's important to be consistent for most of the work on the layout. In some isolated foreground spots, a few trees of a different color can be used for highlights, but for the bulk of the forest and trees, stick to your color system. My system consists of the following ratio of colors: 3 parts medium green, 2 parts dark green, and 1 part light green.

To accomplish this color mix, I build foreground trees in batches of three medium green, two dark green, and one light green. After they are built, forget about their colors and place them randomly. Extreme neatness and regularity will destroy the effectiveness of your scenery, including regular color placement. The key word is "random."

I begin by mixing the colors in a three-pound coffee can with a

Fig. 4. Here are the materials and tools needed to make forest trees: 1. A large coffee can for mixing coarse turf. 2. Assorted shades of coarse turf. 3. Mixed turf. 4. Can of spray adhesive. 5. Bachmann Poly Fibre. 6. Cool Whip container with lid.

Fig. 5. When coating the fiber balls with spray adhesive, use lots of newspaper to catch the overspray.

plastic lid. I dump in bags of Woodland Scenics Coarse Turf ground foam: three of medium green, two of dark green, and one of light green, in mixed color order. I put the plastic lid on the can and shake it for a few minutes. The result is a mixed but uniform color that's compatible with your foreground trees. The color consistency makes the abrupt transition line from trees to forest disappear as shown in fig. 3.

Making forest "trees"

Making "trees" for your forest is simple and many model railroaders have done it. All the same, I don't believe I've ever seen the techniques described in an article.

Figure 4 shows the materials you need: Bachmann's Poly Fibre or a similar material, the can of Woodland Scenics Coarse Turf ground foam colors already mixed, and a can of spray adhesive.

For "tools" all that's necessary is a plastic container with a plastic lid. Be sure it's plastic so the spray adhesive doesn't stick to it. I've found an 8-ounce Cool Whip container works fine. You'll also need a lightweight board, such as a piece of corrugated cardboard or Masonite about 18" square to serve as a

pallet to carry your finished trees to the layout for mounting.

Start by laying a newspaper on the floor against the wall and taping it up the wall. This will be your glue spraying area, and the papers will catch the overspray. As you work the glue will build up on the paper and make it extremely sticky. When this happens, just lay another newspaper over it, and you have a clean work surface. [Check the safety precautions on the adhesive label and heed them. —Ed.]

Tear a small tuft of poly fiber from the contents of a bag and stretch it out into an expanded irregular shape approximating a 2" ball. Lay it on the newspaper and give it a single spray of glue. Turn it over and give it another spray. Don't overdo the glue. If you see the liquid glue beading on the fiber, you have applied too much. See fig. 5.

Place the sprayed fiber in the plastic container and add a handful of ground foam foliage. Put the lid on top. Don't fasten it; just hold it on. Shake the container for about 10 seconds, swirling it so the foam comes into contact all around the fiber. Open the container, and you have a tree. See fig. 6.

Place the tree on your pallet and continue the process until you have

Fig. 6. The sprayed fiber ball is then coated with ground foam by placing both in a plastic container and shaking. Coated fiber balls are in the foreground.

as many trees as you need or until the pallet is full. Don't worry about bare spots on the trees. They can be touched up after the trees are placed. I save the excess foam that collects on the pallet for ground cover needs around the layout and for touch-up on the finished forest.

Placing the trees

I have used several methods for placing the trees on the layout. When I started making this kind of scenery, I used round tapered toothpicks stained in my tie stain. I

Fig. 7. The effectiveness of the author's forest modeling techniques is evident in this photo of a coal extra crossing Altamont Bridge.

sive and sprinkle foliage foam over bare spots. This makes the trees stick together so the forest network remains firmly in place.

The final method is a combination of the first two. I use it on steeply sloped lift-out sections, especially those made from Homasote. I drill 1/16" holes as near to vertical as I can with the lift-out section installed and place the toothpicks in the holes with a dab of white glue. Then I add a light coat of spray adhesive and slip the individual trees down over the toothpicks. I give the trees a light coat of adhesive and fill in the bare spots.

This work is done with the lift-out section off the layout so that the edge trees don't stick to the trees surrounding the opening. For less steep plaster lift-outs sections, I glue the trees directly to the plaster and skip the toothpicks.

Mixing with lichen

If you're like me and your layout has been under construction for some time, you may have some lichen forests in place. I started using lichen but because of the expense and limited availability, I switched to poly fiber trees.

To make the scenery compatible, I sprayed the existing lichen with adhesive and sprinkled my color foam over it. In areas near the foreground I removed the lichen and gave it the full treatment in the Cool Whip container, then replaced it on the layout. To avoid an abrupt transition, I mix the lichen and poly fiber over a distance of a couple of feet, gradually increasing the amount of poly fiber until the lichen is eliminated.

The final step

All that remains is to stand back and look at your work. I'm sure you will be pleased. Over the years we have received more favorable comments about trees and rocks than any other part of the layout. I bet you will too.

mounted them by drilling the plaster with an old 1/16" drill and wedging the toothpick taper into the holes. The holes were spaced at about 2" centers. The trees were placed by stretching them from toothpick to toothpick. After completing about a square foot of forest, I gave the finished area a light spray of adhesive and sprinkled foliage foam over the bare spots in the network.

This method results in a flatter finished texture than the other methods I use. It's good for very large areas that are farther from the tracks and viewers than others. You will get more coverage from your trees this way, but it takes longer than other methods because of the time required for placing toothpicks. The background mountain in fig. 7 was built using this method.

The simplest method, and the one I use most, is to fasten the trees directly to the plaster with the same spray adhesive used to coat them with foliage. Spray an area of plaster big enough for about a half-dozen trees, using a heavier coat of adhesive than you used on the fiber. Immediately place the trees on the glue-coated area; not all will stick. As with the first method, I lightly spray the mounted trees with adhe-

13 In pursuit of better model trees

Thoughts on trees and recipe for home-cooked aspens

Bob Hamm's own HOn3 layout features hundreds of the aspen trees he shows how to make in this article.

BY ROBERT HAMM
PHOTOS BY THE AUTHOR

Before making that first tree you need to consider several topics. These include size, type, appearance, modeling approach, color, and texture. Here I want to present some lessons learned working on my own HOn3 Iron Gorge & Western RR set in the San Juan Mountains of Colorado. I'll conclude by sharing my recipe for making peppergrass aspens.

Tree sizes

Most trees I use in the foreground (aspens, firs, spruces, and others) are between 35 and 40 scale feet (5 to 5½ inches) tall. This is about half to three-quarters the average size of the real thing. I didn't arrive at this size by scientific method, but by simply observing what size trees seemed best to fit my scenery.

I think these smaller trees fit better because many of our structures and scenery features are also undersized. Take structures for example. Often we choose a smaller one not because it's more prototypical, but because it fits the scene better. Often we selectively compress the prototype so it won't overwhelm its surroundings or simply because we don't have enough room for a scale version.

By using increasingly smaller trees towards the backdrop we create the illusion that distances are greater than they actually are. See fig. 1. This technique is called

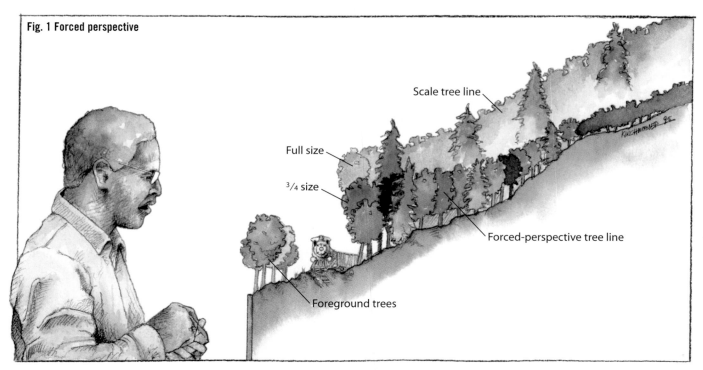

Fig. 1 Forced perspective

Scale tree line

Full size

¾ size

Forced-perspective tree line

Foreground trees

"forced perspective," and it's particularly effective where there are lots of conifers. Their distinctive pointed shapes allow a direct size comparison between background and foreground trees. I go so far as to use background trees that are about one-third the size of those up front.

Tree types and appearance

Geography and climate determine what kinds of trees grow where, and seasons govern how they look at different times. If you're modeling the area where you live, just be observant. Take a few trips over back country roads. Take some pictures, make some notes, and collect some leaves for color samples.

If you don't live in the area you model (as in my case) rely on books, calendars, magazines, and videos. Take a trip to your chosen location, perhaps as a family vacation or as a side jaunt after a business trip. Remember to take your camera.

Generally, I don't try to build specific models of a given species, but I do try to capture the flavor and appearance of the trees of an area.

Try to identify the dominant species. Learn what they look like, how large they grow, where they grow (near streams, on slopes, and so forth) and how they group and mix with other species.

In the part of the San Juan Mountains I model, for example, aspens are the principal deciduous trees, while the conifers are divided among engelman spruce, douglas fir, and lodgepole pine.

Those particular conifers look similar until you get up close and look at the bark and needles, so rather than try to imitate each species, I simply plant several slightly different kinds of tall, conical trees that have the right general appearance.

Selecting tree colors

As you all know, tree color depends on the time of year. For those of us with summertime layouts, it's simply a matter of selecting the right greens. Try to match paint samples with photos or leaves.

In his book *How to Build Realistic Model Railroad Scenery,* Dave Frary suggests using a single base color for your earth. I think it's

similarly important to establish a basic green or group of closely related greens to provide color continuity for deciduous trees and other leafy plants. The conifers also need their own base color.

I use Floquil paints for my final tree colors because they are flat, available in many colors, and easy to alrbrush. I mix three foliage greens all based on Coach Green (RR48) and Burlington Northern Green (RR35).

One mix adds 1 part Reefer Yellow (RR31) to 2 parts of each of the greens, a second adds 3 parts Reefer Yellow, and the last adds 1 part Reefer White (RR11).

Other brands of paint will work as well, but be sure they're flat. Also, in selecting colors be sure to view them under actual layout light.

I keep a notebook of my color samples and mixes, using 8½" x 11" vinyl holders made for 35mm slides. Two-inch-square pieces of white cardboard with the paint samples on one side and the recipe on the other work well.

Foliage texture

When viewed from afar, the best foliage materials have a texture like clusters of leaf-size specks. The more they "pop out" the better the effect.

Another desirable attribute is a delicate or airy structure. You want to be able to look between leaf clusters and see the inner branches.

Fine-textured commercial ground foam when applied to a delicate support armature does a good job of meeting both requirements. I particularly like the AMSI line of ground foams, for both their colors and fine texture.

Many natural materials also have these qualities. Some of the best are: peppergrass (also called baby bush, candy bush, and beige lace), hardhacket (or hardcap), and wild spirea (or meadowsweet). These plants may be known by other names as well.

I buy the peppergrass in florist shops and craft stores, but gather the other materials from overgrown fields and meadows in east-ern New York and Western Massachusetts in the early fall.

All these natural materials are characterized by tight clusters of what appear to be seed pods connected by a delicate armature of branches. The seed pods are about leaf size and generally multi-faceted.

Some of the best-formed weed heads make good trees with little more than trimming and painting. I use wild spirea in this manner for my background trees. Sprigs of the peppergrass work well for aspen saplings and filling in the foreground.

A recipe for aspen trees

Colorado Rockies modelers need aspen trees by the bushel. I build my foreground aspens by gluing peppergrass sprigs to the trunk. Figure 2 shows the tools and materials needed.

For the trunks I use straight twigs or weed stalks ¹⁄₁₆" to ¹⁄₈" in diameter and 3 to 6 inches long. The glue should be thick-bodied and fast drying. Walthers Goo works well, as does Quick Grab by the 3C Co. in Woburn, Mass. A small piece of foam board makes a useful base for setting the tree down.

Typically peppergrass costs $3 to $4 a bunch. Choose the kind that is straw-colored, or "natural." It's most likely to have the "seed pods" that look like leaves. Pick the bunches with the fullest clusters. I've found the quality varies.

Let's build an aspen

The sequence of photos in fig. 3 takes you through the construction, so grab a twig and let's go. It helps to have an image of the tree's basic shape in mind, and that's provided in fig. 4.

I hope you'll give this recipe a try. It works great for me.

Fig. 2 Tree-making supplies. Here's what you need to make the tree shown in fig. 3. The shaker, lower left, contains Highball N scale ballast for adding speckles to the trunk.

Fig. 3. Apply glue to the top ⅔ of the trunk. Cut 30 to 40 leaf clusters ½" to 1½" long while you're waiting for the glue to skin over. Spread these clusters out on a flat surface.

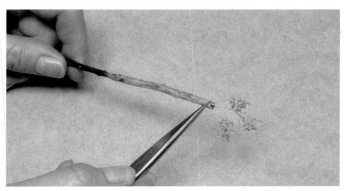

Add a short (½" to ¾" long) cluster to the top of the trunk, sticking straight up. Put the next sprig near it but slightly off vertical. The foliage clusters should touch or come close to touching.

Work down and around the tree in a spiral, using slightly longer (¾" to 1") branches. They should approach horizontal towards the middle branches and begin closing the oval illustrated in fig. 4.

After the cement has set, dribble CA down the trunk to further secure the branches and provide a barrier against the Floquil paint. Then spray the tree basic green.

Once the green is thoroughly dry, paint the trunk and lower branches, varying the color from white to gray. Polly S and other acrylics won't dissolve the green paint and cement underneath.

Now for the *pièce de résistance.* Sprinkle on High Ball N Scale cinder ballast while the white paint is still wet to give the bark a slightly speckled appearance.

Highlight about a quarter of the leaves you can reach easily with a slightly whiter green. This represents the backs of some leaves and gives the realistic illusion that the trees are swaying slightly in the breeze.

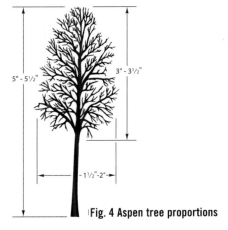

Fig. 4 Aspen tree proportions

Pine trees made quickly and inexpensively from goldenrod dot the hills of Bill Henderson's HO scale Coal Belt RR.

14 Let Mother Nature do it

The Brass Hat turns goldenrod into pine trees

BY BILL HENDERSON
PHOTOS BY THE AUTHOR

Out of Autumn Park Station, passing East Penn Pipe Supply Co. and the Coal Belt coaling tower, the Ten-Wheeler and a string of varnish click-clacked onto the main and into the sun-dappled hills on the way to Tresckova.

"Rats!" said the Brass Hat as he stopped the train. "When a train gets here, the illusion of real railroading vanishes into thin air."

The hills had given way to a barren area of 2 x 4s, plywood, and screen wire. The Brass Hat couldn't stand to have his new brass Ten-Wheeler displayed in these less-than-scenic surroundings.

The chief had been putting off finishing this part of the railroad for over a year while most of the other sections were fully scenicked.

"I want to finish this area with a grove of pine trees, maybe 30 or 40

of 'em, but so far haven't had the gumption to handmake that many trees," he told me.

Having known the Brass Hat for many years, I was sure he would soon have a brainstorm.

Pine trees from goldenrod

Several weeks later I stopped in to check on the progress of the Coal Belt.

"Wait till you see this, Red," he said. "I planted those hillsides with groves of Eastern white pines and it only took two nights."

Indeed, the hills had sprouted miniature trees. The whole area had come alive. "I wouldn't have guessed a few trees could make such a difference," I mumbled through my doughnut.

"A few trees, my foot. There are 41, but I can't claim hard labor because they're so easy to make," he said. "I was walking through the fields last weekend and there they

were: thousands of HO scale trees, growing shoulder-high on long stalks, just waiting to be picked.

"Then and there, I decided to let Mother Nature do it. It's goldenrod, picked in fall after the tops have turned tan and the fine, hair-like fibers are mature (see fig. 1).

"I got about 50 usable plants out of the 100 I picked; some weren't shaped right or the fibers were too coarse. I was careful to leave on several inches of the stem. The stem makes it easy to handle the plant during preparations and will become the trunk of a model tree."

The Brass Hat continued: "I soaked the plants with hair spray to hold everything together, then cut out about half the branches to get the widely spaced branches of real pines (fig. 2).

"I also gave the plants a shot of bug spray to discourage insects from setting up housekeeping on the Coal Belt.

Fig. 1 BEFORE AND AFTER. On the left is autumnal goldenrod as picked; at right is a finished pine tree. All you need for the project are a scissors, candle, pipe cleaner, hair spray, and paint.

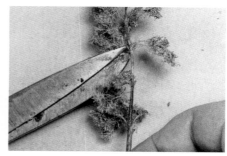

Fig. 2 TRIMMING BRANCHES. Turn the goldenrod into a pine tree by removing about half the branches, opening up the tree until it has the look of a pine.

Fig. 3 TREE TRUNK. Dip a pipe cleaner in candle wax to build up the trunk. Let each coat harden before adding another layer. Finally, paint the trunk and branches gray.

"After the hair spray was dry, I spray-painted the foliage using a green that matched real trees outside. But when I got it inside, the tree changed color under the tungsten layout lights, so I went to a more dense shade of green to compensate—Kmart's Emerald Green, to be exact," he said.

"Well," I said, "all the goldenrod I've been around would give me sneezing fits, and the stalks are really too small to make respectable-sized trunks." I just wanted to hear what he would say.

Tree trunks

Ignoring the thrust of my remark, he went on: "In fall, goldenrod pollen shouldn't be troublesome, and I built up the stalks with melted candle wax.

"I took a pipe cleaner and dipped it into the pool of melted wax that forms around the wick of a burning candle (fig. 3). A large, fat candle works best, and it can be any color because the trunk will be painted.

"Holding the bottom of the goldenrod stem, I used the wax-soaked pipe cleaner to coat it with layers of wax, starting just above my fingers and going up past the lower branches, allowing each coat several seconds to harden. I built up the trunk diameter with successive coats of wax.

"To get bark texture, I took a fine-toothed saw and stroked irregular vertical lines in the wax. To complete the trees, I painted the trunks and limbs Floquil Grimy Black," he added.

The Brass Hat showed me how he had pinched and pulled off some of the fibers, revealing the branch underneath so there was plenty of bark showing.

"You couldn't ask for a better price," I said, knowing Coal Belt management would never buy anything that could be homemade. The Brass Hat believed in saving money to buy locomotives, which he couldn't make at home.

Final details

As a finishing touch, he sprayed the ground under and around the planted trees with hair spray and sifted on brown sawdust to simulate pine straw. "The effect isn't complete without fallen pine needles on the forest floor," he said.

"Why not remind readers to plant pine trees in groups?" he continued. "Although you do find coniferous trees with hardwoods, they are usually growing together in groups or whole forests.

"Conifers are like model railroaders," the Brass Hat concluded. "When you see one, you'll probably see several others as well. They like to congregate."

15 Twisted trees

Modeling coastal live oaks for West Coast railroads

BY MIKE MCCAULEY
PHOTOS BY THE AUTHOR

There are probably as many techniques for producing scale trees as there are types of trees and modelers making them. One of my favorite trees is the coastal live oak. Also called coast live oaks or California live oaks, these trees flourish in western coastal regions from the Pacific Northwest all the way to southern California. The mature trees are tortured mazes of gnarled branches with clumps of dark leaves.

Because I admire these trees, I developed a simple three-step modeling process that uses latex bark over twisted wire armatures to capture their rugged character.

Twisted trees require only a few simple tools and materials; none are critical. I tend to use whatever I have on hand from other projects. You can substitute different brands or types of caulk, paint, or adhesive, either to fit your own style or to use materials you already have.

The armature

The backbone of each tree is a twisted metal armature. I've experimented with types of wire ranging from surplus speaker wire to clothesline. My current preference is for cloth-wrapped florist wire. It takes the latex "bark" better than bare wire, and any frayed ends add extra body or texture to the bark or the foliage.

The wire comes in packages of 18" lengths, with 24 to 30 pieces per package, depending on gauge. Wire packs, which I've found for 99 cents each, are available from most craft stores or florists' suppliers. The 18" length is just right for mod-eling the natural range of heights for coastal live oaks in HO scale.

Twisting wire

Begin by cutting and twisting the wire armature. Cutting the wires in half once and then bending again before twisting yields a scale tree 20 to 25 feet high. I use 5" to 8" wires for smaller trees and 8" to 15" wires for taller ones. Remember that the initial bend gives you two branches for each wire in the bundle.

To make realistic trees, avoid symmetry and cut and group the wires unevenly. Start twisting at the trunk and continue toward the ends of the branches. Over-twist the wires to get the gnarled, tortured look characteristic of these oaks.

When you reach the point where a branch will split off, divide the wires into uneven bundles—about ⅓ of the wires in one and the remaining ⅔ in the other. As you work toward the ends of the branches, try to keep an odd number of wires in each bundle so long as it's feasible.

Bark

Once the armature is finished, use latex caulk and acrylic paint to build up and color it. White and black swirled together with just a touch of brown creates the right shade of gray for coastal live oak bark.

Slather partially mixed caulk and paint over the armature, using enough to obscure the spiral pat-

This shows the various stages of twisting the cloth-covered florist wire for the armature.

An asymmetrical armature will result in a more realistic model oak. Coastal live oaks are twisted, so twist away.

When you're applying the "bark," remember that, in this case, sloppiness is a good thing!

Adding dark-green foliage is the final step—unless you're modeling a foreground tree and choose to add a root structure.

tern of the wire—you want to end up with twists, not candy canes. Don't worry about globs; mature oak tree trunks and limbs are mazes of knots and burls. This is one modeling situation in which sloppiness is necessary.

Once it's dry, I like to add highlighting on the bark by stippling (jabbing or tapping at the tree with a stiff-bristled brush) white paint with an almost completely dry brush. I found that worked better than either using a wash or drybrushing directionally, both of which tended to emphasize the spiral structure of the wire armature.

Foliage

Spray the tree crown with adhesive and dredge it through a pan of ground foam. I found it easiest to get a good load of foliage if I flattened the branches temporarily.

The oaks in my neck of the woods (which isn't called "Thousand Oaks" for nothing) have very dark leaves. Woodland Scenics Conifer Green coarse foliage looks to be about the right color to me.

Use white glue to secure the smaller trees into holes in the scenery base material. For larger trees, I twist a small nail into the armature to use as a planting spike once the tree is finished.

For foreground trees, you can also add roots. Form them by laying a piece of waxed paper over a block of Styrofoam and planting the partially finished tree. Then apply more of the latex/paint mix-

ture down the trunk and onto the waxed paper (the roots don't need to be reinforced with wire).

Once dry, the roots separate easily from the waxed paper. If the tree is to be planted on a slope, or with the trunk at an angle to the ground, remember to insert the trunk into the Styrofoam at the same angle, so the root mass will conform to the slope on the layout.

The finished tree is distinctively true to the prototype. As a bonus, the finished models are almost indestructible and remain flexible enough to be fine-tuned once they're put in place on the layout.

Orange trees and palms line the right of way as Santa Fe no. 2125, an RSD-5, brings home a string of reefers on Charles Nickle's HO Citrus Cove module.

16 Modeling palm trees and orange groves
Realistic trees using grocery store supplies

BY CHARLES NICKLE
PHOTOS BY THE AUTHOR

Palm trees are seen throughout the southern United States, frequently in the same areas as citrus groves. I needed an easy and inexpensive way to model this classic combination of trees on my Citrus Cove HO module. Besides, my local club needed palms to dress up a corner module.

I knew how to make orange trees, but the palms were a problem. Normally I don't model by committee, but when I mentioned my problem at a club meeting, a member suggested palms used by cake decorators. Then another

member thought of a way to alter the leaves to make them look more realistic, and suddenly my dilemma was solved.

If you want to model some of these trees for yourself you will need to shop for supplies in two unusual places. For the orange trees begin at your local supermarket. Buy a pack of long bamboo skewers and several cellulose sponges (7¾" x 4¼" x 1⅜"). Each sponge will make about 15 trees. The rest of the supplies for the citrus trees include dark green latex paint, dark green coarse foam, and a pack of Woodland Scenics red and orange fruit (no. 47).

For the palms, stop at a place

that has cake decorating supplies. Party supply shops and variety stores may carry what you need. Look for toy-like two-trunk palm clusters. Each cluster will make one finished palm. To complete the palms you'll need a pack of beige industrial-style paper towels (white roll-type paper towels will also work), flat tan spray paint, dark green spray paint, and gray and tan acrylic paints.

Making citrus trees

Start the citrus trees by wetting a sponge, then with scissors cut it into three long strips. Next divide each strip into five cubes and trim the cubes into irregular balls (see fig. 1).

When there are enough balls for your grove, skewer each one. Paint with dark green latex paint and coat with ground foam. Let this dry. To patch bald spots, spray with white glue and water mixed with a few drops of liquid soap, then pat on more foam. Sprinkle on the oranges, let everything dry, then seal with another spray of glue and water mixture. Trim the skewers to ¾" long, and they're ready to plant. Drilling a grid of small holes (fig. 1) will produce the corduroy-like rows seen in real citrus groves.

Palm trees

To start the palms, plug in a pencil-point soldering iron. While it heats up, strip all the leaf rings from the two-trunk clusters and throw the trunks out. For each finished palm you'll need to alter three of these rings by just touching the tip of the iron to the stem of each leaf where it joins the ring. This melts the plastic enough to let you adjust the leaf's position by holding it in place until it cools. Three different alterations are needed—see fig. 2.

Next, paint the rings. The straight-down leaf rings can be painted flat tan. Paint the straight-up, unaltered, and half-down rings dark green.

While these dry you can make the trunks. First wrap a bamboo skewer with ⅛"-wide strips of paper towel dipped in thinned white glue. Start at the top, leaving about ¾" bare. For texture, place the saw-tooth edge of the industrial towel strip up (or cut roll-type towels with pinking shears). The closer you wrap the strips the thicker the trunk will be. Leave about ½" bare at the bottom to plant each tree. Real palms vary widely in height, so your models should as well.

When the strips dry, paint them with acrylics, using tan first if you

Charles shopped at unusual places to gather the supplies for this modeling project. A grocery store and cake decorating supply shop were his two stops.

Fig. 1 CITRUS TREE CONSTRUCTION

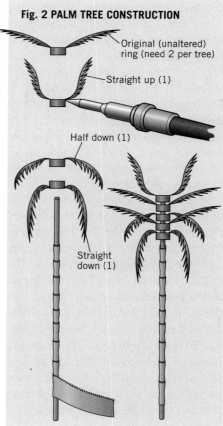

Fig. 2 PALM TREE CONSTRUCTION

Original (unaltered) ring (need 2 per tree)

Straight up (1)

Half down (1)

Straight down (1)

used white towels, then highlighting with gray.

By now the leaf rings will be dry. Thread the rings over the top of the trunk as shown in fig. 2. Secure with a little white glue, trim the top off of the trunk, and touch up the cut end with green paint.

Now you're ready to plant the trees into holes drilled in the layout. That's all there is to modeling this classic combination of trees except for enjoying the compliments!

17 The November scene

Making realistic bare trees with lots of branches

BY PAUL DOLKOS
PHOTOS BY THE AUTHOR

Most model railroaders model summer, so I guess I was being a bit contrary when I decided to represent the beginnings of winter on my northern New Hampshire-based layout.

I had several reasons. First, it would give the railroad a different look. People think of winter as dull and drab, but as I studied it I found an interesting palette of browns, tans, reds, and grays, as well as hardy greens. I also felt that modeling winter would free me from having to create masses of model foliage. Great advances have been made in this hobby, but many of our tree and bush modeling efforts still don't compare favorably with our rolling stock and structures. I thought modeling trees without leaves would open up new vistas.

What probably clinched this line of thinking was a visit to the Harvard University Museum of Forestry in Petersham, Mass. The museum uses 23 large dioramas to depict the changes in the New England forest as the region was settled. These displays include hundreds of accurate handmade tree models that are wonderful to behold. The season depicted is late, fall, chosen so you can see into and through the forest models and study the scenes. A train moving through such a view would be quite appealing.

Speaking practically, these museum tree models set a level of excellence few of us can hope to achieve. The trunks are built of bundles of twisted wire covered with beeswax or solder.

The pine trees have photoetched clusters of needles. These trees are the work of professional model

It's November in New England, and a Boston & Maine local freight is headed south for White River Jct., Vt., on author Paul Dolkos' HO layout. He made the scrub growth along the embankment with many natural materials, including weed tips and ground-up leaves. The fine branch structure on the trees is achieved by gluing sprigs of baby's breath to coarser weed stems. Doug Gurin painted the backdrop.

builders working for Depression-era wages. Given higher labor costs, such a display probably couldn't be duplicated now, but there is a lesson here. We can treat trees and bushes like rolling stock models and consider their shape, size, and color. Then, as practicality and patience permit, we can build them piece by piece and raise the quality of our scenery.

With this idea in mind I proceeded to create a November landscape. Most of the trees have dropped their leaves, carpeting the forest floor, but I also included evergreens for contrast and view blocks.

Starting at ground zero

I use extruded Styrofoam insulation board as the basis for my ter-

rain. It comes in blue or pink, as opposed to the white beaded material, and is lightweight and easy to shape. You can easily poke holes into this foam, which will firmly hold trees or bushes straight without glue or other props.

After shaping the landform, I paint the Styrofoam terrain with earth-colored latex. While it's still wet I sprinkle on some soil or foam ground cover. Some modelers coat the Styrofoam with plaster before painting, but I don't bother unless I'm filling openings or will have bare earth showing in the final scene.

Next, I install the low growth on the forest floor and the taller brush at the edge of the tree line where there's more sun. I use Woodland

Scenics foliage netting, but think it's important to introduce the vertical elements created by upright plants. For this I use small weed tips or anything found in nature that has a fine branch structure. See fig. 1.

Planting is easy—just poke a small hole in the Styrofoam. Sometimes I stick several pieces in the same hole to give the bush some bulk. I also lay in twigs to represent fallen branches and trees. With this variety of materials I'm able to create a thicket of typical brush found in unkempt areas.

Finding appropriately colored foam in autumn and winter hues can be difficult. I've used Woodland Scenics Earth foam and some of the autumn colors offered by Timber Products (2029 E. Howe Ave., Tempe, AZ 85281).

Carpet of leaves

I cover the forest floor with fallen leaves, using ground-up dry leaves gathered in the fall. I place them in a blender, just as you would any vegetable, and puree them. If you try this, add some water or the blender makes a terrible racket. You end up with a pulp that you can spread out on newspaper to dry. If you don't want to use a blender (people seem to cringe when I mention it), you can crumble the dry leaves in your hands, though it may take quite a while to produce a sufficient quantity.

Either way, sift the ground-up leaves through a screen to remove off-size pieces and leaf stems. Sprinkle the scale leaves on the forest floor, and use a brush to position them to your liking. Affix everything by spraying with a mix of water and a drop of detergent to soak the material. Then apply diluted white glue as you would with ballast.

Trees

Now you're ready to add trees. At first I just took twigs that had as fine a branch structure as I could find and stuck them into the Styrofoam base, trying to get them as close together as possible. Because the tops of the trees interfere with each other, it's easy to end up with something that looks more like a park than a forest. You have to interweave the branches to get the close trunk spacing seen in woodlands.

To get the appearance of higher density, in some cases I stuck in a straight twig without any branches to represent a trunk. The thicket of upper branches on the other twigs hides the lack of a top.

You can cover a scene pretty fast, and economically too, because you're using material free for the picking. One of the problems with this approach, though, is that twig ends are blunt, especially after being trimmed to size.

The tops of real trees normally have a network of fine branches. For model trees we can select growth with fine branch structures, but then the lower portion usually isn't thick enough to represent a mature trunk. I alleviated the problem of blunt treetops somewhat by sticking in fine growth among the top branches. This makes a creditable winter forest, particularly if the scene isn't in the layout foreground.

Natural materials

People always ask what natural materials I use. In most cases it's simply what I run across in fields, and I have no idea what the name is, Latin or otherwise. Vegetation is so diverse from region to region that it probably doesn't make sense to recommend certain plants. In fact, some varieties of the same species may be great, while others are useless.

In general, low-growing plants or bushes, as opposed to trees, have the greatest potential for yielding tree and bush-modeling material. Ignore the leaves or

Fig. 1 GROUND COVER. Top: What could make more realistic fallen leaves than the real thing? Paul grinds his up in a blender. Middle: Sprigs of dried weeds picked in the fall make good model vegetation. Some species look best when the dried blossoms are removed. Others, as on the right, look good as is. Bottom: With its fine branch structure, baby's breath, or gyposophila, is good for small bushes or tree branches.

flowers and look at the stem structure. Recently I saw a layout hillside that had been covered with hydrangea blossoms. After the petals had withered, they were removed. The structures that remained made a wonderful forest of leafless trees. Unfortunately, as much as I may want to use this material, I

Fig. 2. DETAILED DECIDUOUS TREES. Top: To create a complex tree armature, glue two or three twigs together. Sometimes you can improve the shape by breaking a branch and setting the fracture with glue. The resulting sharp angle, as seen with one of the branches on the left, is obscured with fine branches added later. Middle: Plaster can be used to fill out the trunk, then start gluing on baby's breath branches. Bottom: The finished tree has been sprayed a dark color (gray-brown) to blend all the pieces.

haven't located a hydrangea bush to harvest.

I have not used any preservatives, but the natural materials I've picked have stood up with little or no breakage. Being mounted in Styrofoam, they are easy to replace if there's a direct hit with a hand or tool.

Another source of material is a florist or craft supply house that handles dried flowers. Here you can purchase dried baby's breath, heather, sugar bush, gypsy blooms, and many others that are good raw materials. Many of them still have blossoms, but if you pick these off you'll end up with what you need. Be aware that the blossoms on growth that's been processed with preservatives such as glycerin are harder to remove than those that have been air-dried. If something isn't the right color, just spray-paint it. Some materials that aren't quite right may be the perfect fill behind some better-detailed trees.

Trees branch by branch

As I worked with the various materials, I began to build a few foreground trees piece by piece, as shown in fig. 2. For the trunk I'd choose a plant that has both a compact branching structure and twig thickness Then I created the network of small branches by gluing on short sprigs of dried baby's breath with the flowers removed.

This process can try your patience, so I usually build no more than six trees at a time. When I have a few minutes, I'll glue on a few sprigs, then go to something else. If you do this each evening for a week, you'll soon have enough foreground trees to populate a large scene.

The trunk and branches end up being different colors, so I spray the assembly with gray Krylon Primer to even it out. Under fluo-

rescent lighting the primer seems to be a reasonable color for bark, which is often more gray than brown. Sometimes I've gone back over the trunks with a wash of brown paint.

We generally don't think much about the scale height of trees because the prototypes come in all sizes, but there's a tendency to make model trees smaller than the prototype. Many trees reach 100 feet at maturity, but my model trees are seldom more than 50 scale feet high. A 100-foot-high tree in HO scale would be more than 12" high and would probably look out of place. Still, where trees are serving as screens or view blocks, we can make them bigger than we do. It's one more factor to consider.

Convincing conifers

Pine trees, at least the ones with the shape of a Christmas tree, are much easier to produce than deciduous species. Any bottle-brush-type armature makes a suitable base. See fig. 3. I've been cutting up the branches of an artificial Christmas tree and trimming them with shears to achieve an appropriate shape and size.

I've also used the branches of a house plant, foxtail fern, which is less dense than a lot of artificial materials. The airiness makes a better-looking tree. See fig. 4. Since you can prune the plant and it will grow new fronds, you're able to continuously replenish your armature supply.

I spray the armature with adhesive such as that sold by Duro or 3M. Then I sprinkle on fine foam, sawdust, or another granular material. This gives the individual branches some bulk.

After spraying on more adhesive I spritz on flock from Vintage Reproductions or Heki, using one of the plastic shaker bottles from these suppliers. Flock consists of fine, short fibers and is often used to represent grass. Flocking gives the tree a prickly or fuzzy look that suggests needles. The look is right, even if the needles are grossly oversized in most scales.

The color of the flock doesn't matter, as I paint the tree dark green with a spray can. You may want to dust the tree with a second color, such as brown, to provide accents. Using this technique you can produce a large number of conifers quickly.

What's next?

Venturing down the road of tree-building discovery, I want to try creating distinct varieties, such as spreading oaks or white birches. True, we usually don't have to worry about particular species, especially if we crowd trees into model forests, but there are areas up front on the layout that deserve a blue-ribbon tree model or two. I think if you approach such a project on a piece-by-piece basis, just as you would a car or locomotive model, you can create that great model tree as well as great scenes.

Fig. 3. CONVINCING CONIFERS. Top: Conifers are easily created using any bottle-brush-type armature. From left, trim to the desired shape. Spray with glue, then sprinkle on foam or sawdust to give the branches bulk. Spray with glue again, and apply flocking to represent needles. Finish the tree by spraying it a dark green. Above: The flocking fibers give the conifer model an appropriate prickly look suggesting needles.

Fig. 4. FOXTAIL FERN. Top: The fronds of a house plant called foxtail fern make an excellent natural conifer armature. Best of all, new fronds will grow to replenish your tree supply. Above: This scene features a pine made from a foxtail fern on the left. Using a variety of materials, including small pieces of weeds and other natural growth, gives woodlands a realistic scrubby look.

18 Add depth to your forests

Using floral shop plants to make a model forest look real

BY BILL HENDERSON
PHOTOS BY THE AUTHOR

The Brass Hat was annoyed. He'd spent hours making a tree-covered hillside and the results stunk. "A can of green paint spilled on the hill would work as well," he snorted. "My trees and leaves are scale and look good close up, but from three or four feet the leaves are too small to stand out."

"Well," I suggested. "If a forest made with realistic components doesn't look real, maybe one that is made with unrealistic components would."

The Brass Hat's eyes lit up like a Hanlon-Buck lantern.

"Watch this," he said as he got out some dyed gypsophila (also called baby's breath) he'd bought from Wal-Mart and sprayed it with a can of Testor's medium green. We cut the gyp tips into pieces about an inch long, coated the stems with contact cement, and stuck them on the original foliage.

The trees came to life, the multi-faceted seeds shimmering and reflecting light in every direction.

Next we decided to try gyp on that old standby, lichen. Success again.

But as we worked higher the effect stopped working. The seeds were too big to suggest leaves at the distance we were trying to portray. Now what?

The Hat's eyes lighted on some candytuft, another floral shop refugee. Could small pieces look like full-size trees on a distant hill? They could, and did, after we spray-painted a few and glued them on the hill's top half.

Next we randomly gave the mountain a few very light spray shots of olive drab and flat black to vary the color.

We sprayed the very top of the mountain with hair spray, then gently puffed on fine green ground foam off a sheet of paper. This smoothed the texture at the top of the mountain where surface detail should be absent.

To further suggest distance, we lightly sprayed the top quarter of the hill with gray primer to suggest haze.

Then the Brass Hat thought how good a row of three-fourth-size candytuft trees would look right behind the track. I gathered several sprigs of painted candytuft into a bunch, taped the stems together, and then covered them with modeling putty to build up a trunk. When the putty dried, I painted it and the small branches flat, dark gray with a small, pointed brush.

If you can't get candytuft in your local floral or craft shops, try Michaels, 1721 Montgomery Hwy. S., Hoover, AL 35244; 705-733-8067.

I thought we were done, but the Hat said we needed a few trees to stand out as individuals, including a few dead trees and a few dark green ones to contrast with the medium green.

"As you know," he said, "I'm modeling 1910, right after the chestnut blight got those dead trees."

Gypsophila, left, and candytuft proved powerful allies in the battle against dull scenery.

Fine ground foam for smooth (distant) texture

Candytuft trees

Area grayed down with a light mist of gray primer

Gypsophila sprigs attached to the tops of weed trees

19 Distant pines
Tree forms to blend scenery and backdrop

BY EARL SMALLSHAW
PHOTOS BY THE AUTHOR

Over the years there have been countless magazine articles on making trees. Most have related to foreground trees, but recently I needed some background trees for my HO Middletown & Mystic Mines layout. I decided to return to a method of creating distant pines that I developed years ago.

Although I model in HO, this technique will work in any scale. Give it a try, and I think you'll find that the process is easy, doesn't cost much, and takes very little time—a combination that's hard to beat!

Start with metal window screen. Older steel screen is best since it bends easily and holds its shape. Cut 3"- to 6"-long strips, 1" to 1½" wide. Use tin snips to cut a row of trees, varying the height of each tree slightly.

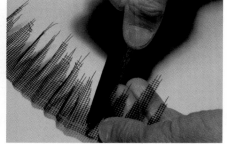

To give a 3-D look, grip the center of each tree with needlenose pliers and bend it slightly. Do this with every tree, then bend the screen the opposite direction between trees. This gives the strip a zig-zag shape.

Coat the strip with white glue. Sprinkle on Woodland Scenics coarse turf, then use Woodland Scenics grass to fill in any voids. Since we don't want these background trees to stand out, keep the colors subdued.

Leaving a 1" gap between the scenery and backdrop allows positioning the tree strips just "over the hill" behind the scenery.

Combine strips of trees, leaving a small space between rows. You can also position some of the slightly taller trees several inches into the foreground.

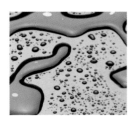

Water

20 Cajon Creek step-by-step
How to model this meandering mountain stream

BY TED YORK
PHOTOS BY THE AUTHOR

I visit Cajon Pass at least twice a year to shoot photographs and collect information for my HO Atchison, Topeka & Santa Fe. In January 2000 I was exploring the pass with Al Bowen, a good friend who is well versed in the history and geography of the area.

My question for him that day was, "Where does the water come from?" Despite the dry desert look of the pass some water always flowed down Cajon Creek. In the many times I'd been there, I had never looked into the creek's sources. Al promptly drove up a narrow road to the north of the tracks; we walked up a short trail where we found a small, clear lake nestled in the center of the San Andreas fault line.

Water seeping up from cracks in the ground formed the lake, providing a source of water flowing through the pass year-round. I was amazed to be standing in a dry landscape looking at more water than I had imagined.

But modeling this water would

A young railfan watches from below as a GP7 helper, lashed to the rear of a Santa Fe freight, crosses Cajon Creek, a year-round source of water.

be a little different from what I had seen on most layouts because Cajon Creek is very shallow and clear, reflecting the color of the streambed itself, varied by shad-

ows from the surrounding rocks, vegetation, and clouds passing overhead. The following photos and captions take you step-by-step through how I modeled my steam.

Ted used a sponge to push the plaster into shape, forming the eroded banks along the riverbed.

After the plaster set, Ted painted it with light tan household latex paint.

Before finishing the creek Ted weathered the bridge and abutments so he wouldn't get the weathering materials on the finished stream.

Preparation

First I prepared the streambed, using cardboard strips to form my scenery base, then attaching cheesecloth with hot glue. Next I painted on two coats of plaster of paris mixed to the consistency of latex paint. To form the final scenery I came in with a coat of casting plaster about the consistency of cake batter.

I formed the smooth areas of the riverbed by spreading the plaster with a spatula, then smoothed it as it set up by simply rubbing the plaster in a circular motion with my hand.

I modeled the concrete under the bridge (the Santa Fe called them concrete blankets) with sheet styrene scribed to represent expansion joints, then installed it with casting plaster.

On many areas along creeks, the bank has eroded leaving the top layers of soil hanging. Modeling this was quite simple with a sponge. I put some plaster on an area, then used a damp sponge to push it toward the bank. As I did, excess plaster moved up and over the sponge. I pushed down upward bulges with my hand, smoothing it out as I did the riverbed.

Dabbing at the plaster with the sponge as it sets up gives the plaster a soil-like texture. After the plasterwork was done I gave it a quick coat of a light tan latex paint.

Then came the fun. I filled paper cups with dirt sifted to various grades and began tossing it over the riverbed. Since my stream was only a small portion of the entire bed and very shallow, I used dirt to form the channel that would contain the water.

I added various shades of ground foam on top of the surrounding banks. Even though I'm modeling the desert there's a lot of plant life, much of it very green in spring.

Next I soaked the material with isopropyl (rubbing) alcohol so the glue would penetrate. I used a coat of diluted Elmer's white glue to fasten the ground cover.

Before working any more on the stream I weathered the bridge and abutments. My weathering materials are on the messy side and I didn't want to get them on the finished "water." I applied a very dilute wash of black shoe dye and isopropyl alcohol on the abutments. I used chalks to streak on the rust and dirt colors that wash down from the bridge. Finally, I painted a thin wash on the bridge, using a very dilute mix of the tan latex paint I used on the plaster.

Painting

Correctly coloring the water-covered portion of the streambed is one of the most important things if you want a realistic-looking stream. I studied photographs of the stream and decided a greenish brown was needed. I used tube acrylics for the project and experimented until I found suitable colors. I painted most of the stream with a raw sienna and white mix, but for the deeper mossy bottom I used an olive green

To give a realistic look to the water Ted painted the streambed with appropriate acrylic paint colors.

Ted drybrushed white where there might be a rapid movement of water, like around rocks and down the concrete blanket.

mixed from black, yellow oxide, and white.

I kept a separate container of water handy to dilute the acrylics as I applied them, watering down the paint as much as I could and still have it cover the dirt. I first painted the riverbed the raw sienna mix, then added the olive color, alternating between the two so I could blend them while wet. I also painted a thin wash of the sienna down the concrete blanket.

Next I drybrushed some streaks of olive down the concrete to give the look of moss build-up where the water flowed over it. Finally I drybrushed some white on areas that might have rapid moving water, such as down the concrete and around rocks. Don't overdo this though, unless you want major rapids.

If you care to add junk to the streambed such as brush, and old tires, now is the time. Let the paint dry before going on to the next step.

Pouring

I used Enviro-Tex Lite two-part epoxy resin for water. The fun thing about this product is that if there's a way for the resin to escape from your streambed it will. I was confident my streambed was leak-proof except for the layout edge.

Sealing this escape route was quite simple: I sandwiched a synthetic sponge between wax paper and a piece of Masonite hardboard. I ran a couple of screws through the Masonite, attaching everything to the fascia and forming a tight seal. The epoxy won't stick to wax paper. Just be sure the dam extends far enough to each side of the stream to prevent epoxy from going around the sides.

The epoxy instructions tell you to pour a maximum thickness of only ⅛". If you need it thicker make separate pours, allowing the epoxy to cure between each. My project took two coats. I used an old brush (old, because it's the last time you'll use it) to direct the epoxy. I also brushed a little on the concrete blanket; I didn't want it to be very thick there. Once I was satisfied with the pour, I left town until morning to avoid the temptation to touch the stuff and mess it up.

Be aware that Enviro-Tex tends to creep up the bank; it also cures as smooth as a sheet of glass. I was modeling moving water and needed ripples, so I bought a small bottle of Gloss-Luster Mod Podge at the local arts and crafts store. Gloss Medium will work as well.

I used a paintbrush to spread the Mod Podge over the cured Enviro-

Sandwiching a sponge between wax paper and a piece of Masonite stops the Enviro-Tex from "escaping" the layout.

Notice how the epoxy has crept into the riverbank along the water. This can be covered with ground foam.

Here's the finished epoxy prior to applying the Mod Podge. It's too smooth to represent moving water.

Ted brushes on several coats of Mod Podge to build up the ripples that are found in moving water.

Tex, pushing down on the brush and spreading the bristles to form a ripple pattern. It took three coats, spread at random, to build up a nice textured surface.

On the concrete I pulled the brush down the slope to get a look of downward movement. After that set up I applied more, this time pushing the brush downward to spread the bristles as I had done with the rest of the stream. I did it several times in the same spots to give the effect of water moving down in sheets as I have often seen on spillways. Although the Mod Podge goes on white, it dries to a nice shine.

Not only does the water now give the illusion of moving down the streambed, it also gave the appearance of distorting the light as I looked into the water. Another nice feature is that if the water starts to look dull after a while, I can just grab the paintbrush and give the stream another quick coat of Mod Podge and it'll be good as new.

21 A tale of three creeks

These waterways illustrate both variety and consistency

Engine no. 28 crosses Fahrens Creek on Jack Burgess' HO Yosemite Valley RR. It's one of the three distinct creeks he models.

BY JACK BURGESS
PHOTOS BY THE AUTHOR

We've all heard that variety is the spice of life. It's easy to follow this advice when adding scenery to our layouts. But if we add a little of this and a little of that, we soon have a mishmash of scenes that don't relate to each other in a realistic way. On the other hand, distinct scenes are essential to helping portray distance and variety.

The solution to this dilemma is to take clues from nature, so slightly different scenes can be developed which will be realistic and also faithful to the prototype.

As my prototype, the Yosemite Valley RR, left Merced in California's San Joaquin Valley and headed for Yosemite National Park, it quickly crossed three creeks: Bear Creek at milepost 1.35, Black Rascal at 1.90, and Fahrens less than a mile later at 2.70.

Regardless of proximity, these crossings are all unique. Bear Creek has relatively uniform banks covered with wild bamboo. Both Black Rascal and Fahrens flow along non-native eucalyptus groves with occasional sycamores or cottonwoods along their banks.

Initial modeling

All three creek crossings have standard YVRR concrete abutments, so I made a mold and cast the six abutments from Hydrocal plaster. I scratchbuilt the bridges from prestained stripwood and n.b.w. (nut-bolt-washer) castings.

Next I installed the bridges and roughed in the scenery with plaster. I used real dirt to form the banks.

The water for Bear and Black Rascal Creeks is casting resin that I poured in layers ⅛" to ¼" deep. Since Bear Creek is relatively deep (a scale 10 to 12 feet), I added color directly to the casting resin, using

Fig. 1 BEAR CREEK. The deep, slow water is perfect for fishing, so Jack added a raft and a youngster whiling away an August afternoon.

Fig. 2 BLACK RASCAL CREEK. To complete the meandering creek scene Jack added a steer and muddy hoof prints.

Fig. 3 FAHRENS CREEK. Detailing on the dry creek bed included adding cattails and bullrushes.

brown and green tints for the first layers and green and blue for the middle layers. The final layers I poured clear. These darker colors emphasize the deep, slow water.

In contrast, just the first layers of casting resin for Black Rascal Creek were lightly colored with green and blue to result in a clear, cool creek.

Once the casting resin had cured, I dappled the surface of the creeks with a coat of acrylic gloss medium.

Bear Creek

I duplicated the dense wild bamboo covering the banks of the real Bear Creek using Woodland Scenics field grass (fig. 1). I applied it by cutting small clumps and gluing it in place with white glue. This was tedious but produced the look I was after. While there is a tendency for the material to lean over, just keep pushing it up. As the glue dries, it will finally hold position. Using sticky white craft glue rather than regular white glue also helps.

Once the bamboo was in place and the glue had dried, I used a moustache scissors to trim the material to a relatively even length.

Since the banks of Bear Creek were covered with bamboo, little further detailing was needed.

Black Rascal Creek

In contrast to Bear Creek, Black Rascal (fig. 2) is more typical of the meandering creeks draining the foothills in the Merced area. Moisture in the adjacent ground allows the grass to remain green during the hot summer months.

To duplicate these conditions, I airbrushed Noch electrostatic grass a light green. The willows which encroach into the creek are a combination of Woodland Scenics field grass with flower pieces from dried artichoke heads dyed light green. (Dried artichoke flowers can be found in craft stores.)

Since the area next to the bridge seemed an appropriate watering hole, I mixed diluted white glue with fine-grained clay soil and spread it on the banks. I gave the muddy area a light coat of acrylic gloss medium to make it look wet.

Fahrens Creek

Unlike Bear and Black Rascal Creeks, Fahrens (fig. 3) modeled as a dry creek bed, typical of the Merced area in mid-summer. I used Woodland Scenics field grass to model the bullrushes along the creek banks, hot-gluing it in place

Cattails were made with short pieces of fishing monofilament which had been dipped in white glue and allowed to dry to form the heads. I then painted the heads brown.

I used fine beach sand to form the creek bottom and bonded it in place with diluted white glue. The sand was added after the field grass was in place, covering the hot glue.

Portions of the real Fahrens Creek banks are covered with wild blackberry vines. To model this, I started with small poly fiber balls covered with ground foam, bonded the foam with hair spray, and glued them in place with white glue. A light sprinkling of red foam replicated ripening blackberries.

Modeling scenery accurately requires no more than observing nature and, sometimes, developing techniques to reproduce what you observe. Detailing scenery can be a relaxing diversion from working on the rest of the layout.

22 Lily pads, cattails, and pond scum
Techniques for modeling freshwater pond details

BY GERRY LEONE
PHOTOS BY THE AUTHOR

Even if you're not modeling my home state, the Land of 10,000 Lakes, your layout may have a lowlands area that could use a small lake, pond, or bog. These shallow, quiet bodies of fresh water usually contain cattails, lily pads, and pond scum. Here are a few simple techniques for modeling those details.

Two shakes of a cat's tail

Cattails are common perennial herbs that grow anywhere from 5 to 9 feet high. Modeling cattails takes several steps, but the process lends itself to making dozens at a time.

In HO, use Plastruct .010" plastic rod cut into approximately 1" lengths for the main stalks. To color the rods, hold them with tweezers and dunk each into a bottle of Polly Scale 404076 Coach Green—a color that blends in nicely with Woodland Scenics ground foam colors. Let the stalks dry thoroughly.

Cut a small tab, about 6 scale

Fig. 1 CATTAILS. Shown in the inset is the prototype—full-grown cattails in summertime. To model the basic stalk, cut a small tab in a piece of paper to paint nail polish on Plastruct rod. A book holds the tab in place as you work.

inches across, out of a piece of heavy paper. This will be your paintbrush for creating the cattail's velvety brown seed pod. Using the pages of a book to hold the tab above your workbench, put a sizable drop of brown nail polish on the end of the tab.

Wait a minute or so for the nail polish to thicken. Hold the Plastruct rod parallel with the paper

painting tab and drag about 6 scale inches of the tip through the polish, creating a blob (see fig. 1). As you drag, roll the rod between your fingers to distribute the polish evenly. Poke the rod into a small scrap of rigid foam to dry.

Be careful not to use too much nail polish—not only will the cattail be oversized, but the enamel in the nail polish will weaken the plastic. For fat cattails, it's better to use two thinner coats and let the polish dry in between.

If your blob is too bulbous or poorly shaped, let it dry for a minute or two and reshape it by gently rolling it on the surface of your workbench or between your fingers.

Once the polish hardens, dip the top of the cattail into Polly Scale 414275 Roof Brown.

The final step is to paint the top 6" spike of the cattail, again by tweezer-dunking. The color on this end varies: in mid-summer it's a vibrant rust orange (Polly Scale 414323 Rust), but as fall nears the color changes to beige (Polly Scale 414317 Concrete).

Green and gold grasses

I use Enviro-Tex Lite two-part epoxy to model water. It's easy to work with and its surface dries completely level—perfect for small, still bodies of water such as woodland ponds.

Your shoreline and shallow water should contain an abundance of the tall grasses cattails grow in. I mix Woodland Scenics medium green, dark green, and gold tall grasses to achieve the effects of new, mature, and dead vegetation, respectively. Use white glue to cement pencil-diameter-sized bundles to the shore as well as out several scale feet onto the water surface. It's best to space the initial plantings widely apart; once the glue dries, I can plant more, getting the vegetation as dense and even as possible.

It's easiest to plant most of the grasses before pouring the resin. Once the Enviro-Tex has set, go back and use white glue to attach a small amount of additional grass in front of that already planted. This hides the areas where the Enviro-Tex has crept up the stems of the grass bunches.

Cut your cattails slightly shorter than the tallest grass, and use a

Fig. 2 LILY PADS. Water lily plants grow in great multicolored clusters in larger bodies of freshwater. Gerry used a sharpened piece of brass tubing to punch out lily pads by the dozen.

droplet of cyanoacrylate adhesive (CA) or white glue to plant them among the grasses.

Lily pads with a punch

Lily pads—the leaves of water lily plants—flourish along the shallow shorelines and quiet inlets of larger bodies of fresh water. The 6"- to 15"-broad leaves are medium-green when young, dark green when mature, yellow while dying, and brown once dead. Many leaves contain several colors. Lily pads usually grow in great abundance, with the leaves often overlapping one another as the plants fight for sunlight.

The easiest way to model lily pads is to punch them out—literally—by the dozen. First, put several drops of Polly Scale 414122 Reefer Yellow, Coach Green, and Roof Brown on a piece of white paper. Use a paintbrush to mix, overpaint, and push the colors around the paper at random. Then let the paint dry completely.

To make the lily pad punches, chose several short lengths of brass tubing with inner diameters ranging from 1/16" to 1/8". Use an awl or nail set to flare the end of each tube slightly and chuck it into a variable-speed electric drill. Run

the drill at slow speed while holding a round needle file in the open end of the tube. In a minute or two you'll have a sharp cutting edge.

Now the fun part. Put the painted paper on a soft surface such as a cutting mat, and punch out your lily pads. Depending on the thickness of your paper, you may need to tap the back end of the punch with a hammer. (See fig. 2.) If you'd like to give the lily pads the characteristic "dinner plate" shape, punch six to ten at a time, and poke them out of the tube from the back with a piece of stiff wire or a toothpick. The slight flaring of the end of the tube will cause the lily pads to become slightly concave as they stack up inside.

Cut the characteristic stem slot in each of the lily pads with a sharp hobby knife, then glue them to the surface of your pond, making sure to randomly overlap their edges.

Pond scum

In summer, the combination of heat, humidity, and sunlight is perfect for the development of scum on small bodies of water (fig. 3). This green scum actually comes from one of two biological sources: algae and duckweed. It's most prevalent on smaller ponds,

Fig. 3 SCUM. Algae and duckweed can completely cover the surface of a small body of water in late summer. In a model, the sheer amount shown in the inset photo would be overkill.

Floquil 110048 Coach Green directly onto the surface, right next to the shore. Over the next hour the paint will spread an inch or so, turning from solid green into a network of extremely fine green flecks. The result is a convincing scum that's part of the surface and can't be damaged.

When choosing your scum color, be sure to compensate for any tinting you added to your Enviro-Tex, as this will affect the final color. If you space your initial paint dabs far enough apart, surface tension and drying will keep them from mixing together. This will form convincing "critter trails" to the shore.

Dressing up a small lake, pond, or bog can be an interesting modeling diversion. Some would even call it a quiet refuge (pun intended) from the daily demands of a layout!

A special thanks to Dr. Dick Osgood, good friend and limnologist, for some of the technical details in this article.

although it does accumulate on the windward shores of larger bodies of water.

If your pond is already in place, sprinkle fine ground foam (Woodland Scenics Weeds or Grass works well) along the shoreline and use diluted white glue or matte medium to secure it to your Enviro-Tex water.

If you have yet to pour your pond, try this. After the Enviro-Tex has set for about 45 minutes, use a toothpick to dab small droplets of

Dioramas as opportunity

A small diorama is a powerful tool for modelers. It's certainly useful as a testing-ground for techniques we're curious about or want to practice, as Gerry showed here. Also, it can give us an opportunity to model details that we're dying to try but just don't have any place for on our layouts. What if your layout is based on a '50s-era Midwestern railroad, for instance, but you've always had a craving to model one of those great wooden trestles characteristic of early 1900s logging operations in the Pacific Northwest? A stand-alone diorama might be the ideal solution.

Gerry discovered another hidden benefit of dioramas—they're portable. Several times, he took this one to his office, set it on his desk, and found it worked wonderfully as a conversation piece—he got lots of co-workers asking if they could come over to see his layout. For any

model railroader who wants to be an ambassador for the hobby, this alone might be a great reason to build an attractive diorama. You might take it to other places where lots of people could see it—church socials, club meetings, schools, or your public library.

Gerry told us he tried 14 new techniques on the diorama—including

handlaying track, which he'd always wanted to try. After handlaying the 18″ of track on this diorama, he says with a chuckle that he likes to tell his model railroader friends he's handlaid an entire layout! This news is often received in respectful silence. And then he adds the kicker: "And I did it in a single evening!" —*Mike Johnston, senior editor*

23 Modeling Waterfalls

Using clear plastic and silicone sealant to represent cascading water

BY GEOFF NOTT
PHOTOS BY THE AUTHOR

I find forests and the water that flows through them inspirational. Fast-flowing streams, cascading waterfalls, and lush, abundant foliage provide fantastic subjects to model. In building my HOn3 Leigh Creek Lumber Co. layout, which has extensive waterfalls and water areas, I have tried many published methods for making waterfalls. Some of these methods are difficult and hard to control, so gradually my techniques have evolved to become as quick, simple, and realistic as possible. The following photos provide a step-by-step look at how I create these effects. They can be done in any modeling scale.

Geoff Nott's On3 diorama features many fine examples of waterfalls and rushing water.

1. When modeling waterfalls, I've found the best results are achieved by breaking the descent of the stream into a series of smaller falls of varying heights, each of which drop into different-sized ponds. Set up the falls and pond areas by building a series of flat, smooth shelves made of hardboard or plywood. Make sure each is level. These boards can also be glued directly onto existing scenery.

2. Prepare the waterfall material at your workbench. Start with pieces of stiff (at least .015") clear plastic, cut slightly larger than needed for each section of falls.

Apply clear silicone sealant to the plastic in a narrow line and spread it downward with a piece of stripwood. Drag excess sealant to the bottom, past the edge of the plastic. Repeat this until the plastic is covered. I try to work the sealant quickly, as it can become lumpy as it dries. I aim for a fine, textured finish.

When the surface is dry, drybrush the textured sealant surface with white acrylic paint. Use a fine brush and begin very lightly, wiping most of the paint off of the brush and then stroking it along the surface. Build up the color slowly. For gently flowing falls I try to paint varying patterns of falling water. More texture in the sealant and more paint will produce a raging water effect.

3. The flat boards are used as a base for pieces of real rock (I use shale) or rock castings. Glue them in place with a brown gap-filling adhesive such as latex Liquid Nails. A variety of shapes is important. I like to install a rock which protrudes from the top of the falls so the water has a clear drop to the base of the falls, rather than having the water flowing down a rock face.

For ground contours surrounding the rock I use chicken wire, which allows great flexibility in shape. Cover this with a layer of paper towels coated with full strength white glue, followed by several layers of newspaper strips coated with glue. (I find plaster messy and have eliminated it from my modeling.)

4. Complete the rock strata with small pieces of rock glued in place. Arrange loose and fallen rocks at the bottom of the falls, rapids, and rock faces. Add foliage, logs, and other debris around the falls and water areas, and secure them with diluted white glue (one part glue, three parts water, and a bit of dish detergent).

5. Trim and position the finished plastic strips to form the falls. Use small dabs of clear sealant at the top and bottom to hold the strips in position.

6. Make a misty spray effect by teasing out white poly fiber (found in craft shops). Roll the fiber in your fingers and tease it out for fine application.

Add a coat of artist's acrylic gloss medium to the strips of plastic—this gives the poly fiber something to stick to—then press the fiber into place.

Don't try to add gloss medium to the fiber.

At this time you can also add more foliage around the falls to help blend the scenery together.

7. Use a small, stiff coarse-bristled brush to stipple thick white texture paint over the smooth pond areas to achieve waves and other moving water effects.

Once this dries use artist's acrylic paint to color the water. I prefer green tones for mountain streams, painting dark green over light green for highlights in some areas.

8. Brush and drybrush some white paint at the bottom of the falls and rapids. Use a fine brush to highlight the tops of the waves out in the pond.

9. Add a coat of gloss medium over the painted surface to create the effect of sparkling water.

10. Make the water descending through the rocks by spreading clear silicone sealant through these areas. Rough up the sealant surface to simulate fast-flowing water. Very rough water at the base of the rapids can be modeled by teasing and shaping the sealant into waves. Thick modeling paste will also work.

Drybrush white acrylic paint over the sealant to represent foam and rushing water. Apply the paint sparingly so some of the clear sealant shows through.

11. Finish the rough water areas with a coat of gloss medium.

12. The waterfall is now complete, with the mountain stream cascading down the rocks and rapids into the pond.

24 Modeling surf and sand

Capturing the look of Santa Fe's Surf Line is easier than you might think

Santa Fe's warbonneted stainless-steel F units lead the San Diegan north along the sun-drenched beach of San Clemente in the summer of 1953.

BY KEN PATTERSON
PHOTOS BY THE AUTHOR

I built this HO scale diorama specifically as a photo prop. Such projects give me the chance to do a wide variety of modeling and experiment with different techniques without committing myself to them as I would if they were on a layout.

I'd already decided I wanted to try a summer beach scene before I really knew where, or even if, there were prototypes for beach-side railroads, so the first order of business was research. Where do real trains run along a beach? Could I include sunbathers and fun beach scenes? Should I even attempt to model the ocean?

Scenes like this Amtrak *San Diegan* on the Surf Line inspired Ken's Modeling efforts. Photo by Bruce Kelly.

Even after adding figures I felt something was missing. A sandcastle! After several experiments with building one grain by grain, I used a Woodland Scenics automotive engine block lying on its side. When painted with my sand colors, it looked perfect.

I spread a little plaster over the smooth foam board to form the parking lot and covered the rest of the surface beyond the tracks with ground foam. The riprap is a commercial stone product (I've lost the bag and don't remember the manufacturer) poured over white glue I'd brushed on the slope. The steps are from Central Valley.

The finished ocean. Note how waves tend to form a staggered pattern, almost like brickwork, with an inshore wave overlapping a break between waves farther out.

I started searching all of my back issues of *Model Railroader* to see if anyone had modeled the surf or a beach with a train on it. The only train-and-beach photo I found was one by Peter Youngblood in the December 1979 issue. The caption identified it as the Santa Fe's oceanfront line running along the beach near San Clemente, Calif. Although Peter didn't model the water, it was a great photo. I'd found my real-life beach railroad.

Next came the search for prototype photos of San Clemente. Wow! I found ten in various books, including a great shot in the Kalmbach book *The Spirit of Railroading* [out of print], page 180. This photo by David R. Busse was my starting point for the model.

I decided to include the following: a train, the parking lot, the old ATSF San Clemente station, the sunbathers on the beach, and the surf.

Before modeling anything, I set up the camera so I'd know what it would see. As a result, I didn't model the station, as it wouldn't show in the photo.

I was quite happy when my efforts were rewarded by Walthers purchasing the photo for its summer brochure. But I'm even happier that this project turned out so well that I'll probably use it on the Midwest Valley Modelers modular layout.

The photo captions will take you step by step through my modeling of track, sand, and ocean.

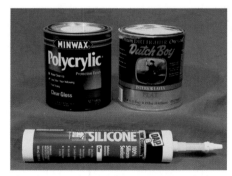

Here's what I used for my ocean: dark blue latex paint (I used flat, not gloss), silicone caulk for the foam on the surf, and a clear gloss overcoat from Minwax to make the water look wet.

Surf 'n' sand step-by-step

1. I used a Stanley Surform to contour the beach sand area, purposely leaving a rough surface on the sand. When I was happy with the shape, on went tan latex house paint for the beach and dark blue for the ocean. I wasn't too choosy about the blue as I was shooting outdoors and counted on the blue sky to help give color, just as it does to the real ocean.

2. I highlighted the rough surface of the sand by airbrushing Floquil Earth at a low angle. Woodland Scenics fine brown ground foam worked perfectly to represent dead seaweed washed up on the beach. This important detail adds life to the beach by marking the high-tide waterline.

3. The surf was fun and easy to create. I squeezed clear caulk in a series of arches along the beach to model the crests of breaking waves. A good high-angle picture of the ocean or looking at the real thing will help get this right.

4. Behind the crest of a breaking wave is a trail of foamy water, made by pulling the back side of the waves smooth with my finger.

5. To create the effect of the heavier surf farther from shore, I made the water cascade over itself by pulling up the partially set caulk with my finger.

6. To hide the area where the beach meets the blue water, I used white house paint to create a foamy look. I also used this same white paint to enhance the top of all the waves in the scene.

Backdrops

Improving commercial backdrops

Ways to personalize the world beyond your layout

Author Greg Condio eliminates the repetitiveness of printed backdrops by cutting away their skies, adding signs, and pasting them on top of one another.

BY GREG CONDIO
PHOTOS BY JIM CUNNINGHAM

By placing a printed backdrop against a blue wall behind our layouts, we achieve distance, perspective, and a sense that the scene exists somewhere in the real world. The problem? Use the same backdrops more than once and your world gets repetitive.

Here are some techniques I use on my HO scale Baltimore & Ohio RR to give my backdrops individuality and make them stand out.

Buildings away

Starting with Walthers Hotel/ Business Instant Horizon printed backdrop no. 949-712, glue it to a four-ply mat board using 3M spray-mount adhesive (sold at photo and art stores). When it's dry and not tacky (the glue, not the backdrop), cut the sky away from the buildings using a sharp hobby knife. See fig. 1.

Look through magazines, news-papers, business cards, and cou-pons for advertisements to apply to the cut-out buildings. These will give the viewers' eyes something to focus on so they'll overlook the

77

Fig. 1 REMOVE THE SKY. Use a straightedge and a sharp hobby knife to separate the sky from the buildings. Chicken Little would be proud of you.

Fig. 2 SIGN HERE. Cut advertisements from magazines, newspapers, business cards, and coupons and glue them to the backdrop to add individuality.

repetitive parts of the backdrop. After you find an appropriate advertisement, cut it out and glue it to a backdrop building.

When you're through adding ads, glue the first backdrop to the wall, about 1″ above the horizon, using spray mount on the back of the buildings, not the sky backdrop. Add the second backdrop in front of the first for depth. It's best to play around with how these work with each other before gluing them in place.

For the ultimate in individuality for your backdrops, go outside and photograph your local city or town. Take the resulting slides or negatives to a photo shop and have them enlarged so that they fit your scene.

26 Photo-realistic backdrops

You can substitute your camera for artistic skill

**BY DOUG TAGSOLD
PHOTOS BY THE AUTHOR**

Early in my modeling career I discovered there was a big difference between how I'd like my backdrops to look and how I was able to make them look with a paintbrush. Then I had an idea. Why not use blown-up photos for the backdrops and use the time I would have spent painting to work on something else? I've been doing that ever since.

The 20″ x 30″ enlargements I use are called Giant Posters, and they typically cost between $15 and $20 each. Yes, one print costs more than a gallon of paint, but remember, after I've glued a print to a section of backdrop, that section is

finished, quick and easy. And unlike paint, you never need a second coat of Giant Poster.

When I was in Colorado, I knew it would be a long time before I'd be able to return, so I spent a few dollars for an extra roll of film. I wanted to be sure I had all the photos needed to make backdrops for the model railroad I was planning to build.

The first shot

The most difficult part in shooting a backdrop is finding a place to stand where you can get a wide view of the scene without something in the way.

It helps to know how large an area you want a series of photo-

graphs to cover. Knowing the enlarged photos would be 30 inches wide, and allowing for some overlap, I figured each shot I took would make 2 feet of backdrop. For the mountain scenes, I took several series of photos using different lenses. The results can be seen in the photo on the opposite page.

I took my first shot with a 50mm lens, starting from the far left of the scene and noting some landmark near the right side of the view. I then panned to the right until that same landmark was near the left edge of the view through the camera. This ensured that the photos would overlap a little. I repeated this process until I reached the end of the scene to the right.

It took four photos with the 50mm lens to cover the scene, which means at roughly 2 feet per photo, this would make a backdrop about 8 feet long. Next I shot the same scene while using a 180mm telephoto lens. Because the telephoto lens has a narrower field of view, the pan required 10 photos to cover the same scene.

Thinking I might never come back again (though I have—twice so far), I shot the scene over using the zoom lens at 80mm and at 120mm, just in case the first ones turned out to be too big or too small. As it turned out, all were just fine.

Size isn't always important

For distant scenery, the size of the mountains didn't matter much. The trees on the photos taken with the 180mm lens approached HO scale. The other photos just looked more distant. The scene on my layout behind Big Ten Curve and Plainview required a backdrop 20 feet long, so I used the photos made with the 180mm lens. Other photos were used for backdrops on other sections of the layout.

I've used different photo backdrops, including the Rio Grande's North Yard. For this series of shots I found an area overlooking the yard from about a half mile away with an unobstructed view. This is important because an object close to where you are standing, such as a car, building, or utility pole, will appear over scale when enlarged.

When size is important

You should be careful to get the subject the right size anytime there are man-made objects in the scene. The day I was shooting, the yard had several auto racks waiting to be loaded. Knowing the final size of the enlargement, 30 inches, or 2½ feet, and guessing that in HO scale an auto rack was about 12 inches long, I zoomed my lens in and out until I had 2½ auto racks in the camera's viewfinder. This

Rio Grande freight no. 187 climbs the Rockies west of Denver. Doug Tagsold's backdrop looks real because it's a photo of the real thing.

Scale table

Distance from subject for taking photos in scale to be enlarged to 20" x 30".

Camera lens	N scale	HO scale	O scale
28mm	335 ft.	180 ft.	100 ft.
35mm	375 ft.	203 ft.	113 ft.
50mm	600 ft.	326 ft.	180 ft.
100mm	1,200 ft.	650 ft.	360 ft.
150mm	1,800 ft.	775 ft.	540 ft.
200mm	2,400 ft.	1,300 ft.	720 ft.

would make the racks 12 inches long in the enlarged photo.

To be safe, I reshot the entire series with the cars a little larger, and then a little smaller. I used up an entire roll of film, but that was cheaper than buying a plane ticket to come back to Denver. As it turned out, my first guess was the best and I used the shots with 2½ auto racks per print.

Installation

I always cut the "sky" out of the photos before installing them on the backdrop because it's difficult to hide joints between photos in the sky. I make my own sky by painting the backdrop blue and painting in clouds. They give the finished backdrop scene a three-dimensional effect. For more on figuring distance from a subject for a 20″ x 30″ print, see the accompanying table.

Before putting up the first poster, I look at the scene to see from which angle it will be viewed most often. If it will be viewed mostly from the right, I install the posters starting from the scene's left end. That way the overlapping edges of the posters will be away from the viewer, making them less noticeable. If the scene will be viewed most from the left, I begin at the right.

On an area where the scene will be viewed from the center I install the posters starting from both ends. This takes extreme care in measuring beforehand to be sure the two scenes come together where they're supposed to.

I use contact cement to mount the photos, following the instructions and placing the cement on both the backdrop and the backs of the photos. I could have used an extra pair of hands, because once the poster touches that backdrop, it's stuck. It's got to be right the first time.

I recommend using a dehumidifier in your layout room during the

This yard backdrop is composed of a series of 12 poster prints, running the full 25-foot length of Doug's model yard.

Southbound Santa Fe freight no. 424 passes through the rolling hills near Castle Rock, Colo. Matching the foreground scenery with that of the backdrop gives the illusion of great depth though the scene is only 16 inches deep.

more humid months. I haven't had any problems with curling or peeling since I started using contact cement, but still, I'd rather not take any chances with the photos.

A few tips to remember

An important thing to know is that "Giant" or "Big Print" posters are meant for viewing from a distance. If you look at them up close, you can see they're not quite as sharp as smaller prints, but from a few feet away they look fine. If you want an enlarged photo with sharper detail, you'll have to pay more.

One more suggestion: Make sure to have all the prints processed at the same time. On one occasion, I

took some in at one time, then the rest a few weeks later. The two groups of photos didn't match in color because they didn't go through the same chemicals at the same time. To help blend the color of the prints together, I had to lightly over-spray them with an airbrush.

If you're not sure about the idea of using photos for your backdrop, try it on a small scene first, or perhaps try adding a photo of a structure to your existing backdrop. Don't be surprised if the effect leaves you wanting to do more. For me, there's no better way of bringing the real world to my layout, especially when I want specific scenes or structures that would be difficult or impossible to model.

27 Landscaping by guess (and by gosh)

How to blend three-dimensional modeling into the backdrop

BY BILL HENDERSON
PHOTOS BY THE AUTHOR

You were probably amazed, as I was, the first time you saw how much better models looked in scale surroundings. More than just a prop, a scenic setting provides the scale for comparison. Good scenery enhances even so-so models, and since some of my home-built engines suffer from that malady, I've always tried to make up in landscaping what I lack in locomotive modeling skills.

My approach to landscaping on my HO scale Coal Belt RR is visually literal—I like to see every blade of grass. I try to model the miniature natural world as it would appear in full scale as seen in a photograph.

This approach calls for a realistic backdrop. At one time I had the mistaken notion I could paint the masterpiece, but the evidence that accumulated on the wall pointed to an abysmal lack of talent. Instead of giving the trains mass and scale, it simply said, "This is as far as the world goes, bub. The room wall starts here."

However, I did have enough talent to cut photos out of magazines, large-format landscape books, and calendars. I used contact cement to glue the cutouts to thin, stiff cardboard, cut off the sky, then gave the pieces a misting of Testor's Dullcote.

Here are four scenes that illustrate how I blended these backdrop cutouts with the scenery on my layout to create seemingly seamless scenes.

Field and farmhouse

In this integrated scene, there's no obvious division between the three-dimensional scenery and the backdrop. The scene started with a ridge, field, and farmhouse photo cut from a calendar. I extended the pictured field down to the tracks in three dimensions, a distance of 8". I spray-painted poly fiber (a material used in quilts and pillows, available at sewing and crafts stores) randomly with brown, green, and tan to match the tile picture, then pulled it apart into patches and laid it over a wire screen landform up to and overlapping the bottom edge of the photo. The poly fiber grass provides a transition between the picture and the scenery and masks the compression of the modeled field.

Where it meets the backdrop photo, the fiber is pulled apart until it resembles a spider web. This results in a grass mat that doesn't show individual fibers, but blends into the image.

To enforce the feeling of distance, I used spray-painted nylon scouring pads, which I had pulled

Poly fiber "grass" helps blend the farm field on the backdrop with the more detailed scenery behind the tracks.

and stretched, and synthetic steel wool grass patches as the field approached the tracks. I use 3M medium coarse synthetic steel wool. (Don't use regular steel wool, as stray steel fibers can damage

motors and bearings.) The material is available at paint stores.

To further enhance the effect, I very lightly, and in one quick pass, sprayed gray primer on the ridge to put some haze into the scene.

River and banks

Looking at the backdrop water in the photo above, you'll notice it appears to run uphill. This illustrates a problem with backdrops. If the horizon is the correct height to show proper perspective for standing operators, then there's a distortion of perspective when photographing trains at track level. A low, wooded ridge turns into Pike's Peak when you're looking at it from a low vantage point. The same thing happened to the creek, but from a standing eye level it appears to run toward the background.

Tall benchwork minimizes this distortion, but it's not practical for everyone. I compromised and tried to cover all bets by locating my horizons about 3" or 4" below my standing eye level.

I glued the photos to the sky backdrop at various places behind the tracks, and using wire screening covered with plaster, modeled the three-dimensional land forms as if they were extensions of the ones shown in the pictures. The modeled creek was extended from the pictured creek toward the front of the benchwork, with its size and direction determined by the rocky banks shown.

Rotted wood rockwork. The photo that I glued to the backdrop shows tilted stratified rock bluffs on both sides of the brown-green water. After preparing a plaster streambed, I painted it with brown and green acrylic paint to match the photo and later poured in ¼" of clear polyurethane varnish in several layers.

To hide the joint between the photo and the modeled water, I extended the pictured rocks in the streambed using small chunks of rotted wood from a fallen tree I found in the woods. To confuse the observing eye, I also glued several chunks to the photo in the vicinity of the rocks. I used bigger slabs to model three-dimensional bluffs as forward projections of those shown on both sides of the creek.

Selecting wood slabs that looked like those in the picture was no problem because bark and pieces of fallen trees come in an amazing variety of patterns and surface textures. Most have already been colored by nature to match colors of real rock. I tinted the wood pieces with a wash of brownish-gray acrylics.

If you use this lazy person's rockwork, spray it with bug spray to get rid of unwanted visitors, then seal it with hairspray or Dullcote before using.

Vegetation. The "by guess" in the title of this chapter means I'm never sure what the scenery will look like until it's finished due to my habit of experimenting with various materials. But, by gosh, sometimes I do wind up with the scenery I had pictured in my mind, even if it takes three or four attempts.

I filled in the bare spots and crevices between the wood slabs and the screening to which they were glued with spray-painted poly fiber (Woodland Scenics also makes poly fiber, already dyed green).

Poly fiber was too fine to simulate the boggy growth of the moss,

Blending the rotted-wood rockwork and varnish water surface with the backdrop was the key to realism in this scene.

grasses, and brush that grow near water and damp rock outcroppings. However, floral moss is just the ticket to fill up space with rank growth.

I also wanted vines and brambles in this scene, and used more of the 3M synthetic steel wool. Because the fibers of these materials are larger in diameter than those of poly fiber, they do stand out as individual blades and stems of simulated grass and brush.

As with poly fiber, I yanked, jerked, tore, stretched, picked apart, and pulled the synthetic steel wool into small ragged patches or loosely clinging clumps. Some I glued flat on the surface and some I sat on edge in bunches, any way to obtain variated surface texture in irregular patterns.

A few sprigs of peppergrass, some pieces of dried moss, and seedheads of actual grasses found in fields and roadside ditches completed the scene.

Railroad embankment and hill

The fill and the hill it joins are window screen covered with plaster. I painted it with brown latex paint and sprinkled on screened soil. Good sources of soil are ballfields and dirt roads. After drying, it can be poured through

screen or a tea strainer to remove lumps, then poured through nylon stockings or cheesecloth to sift out the powder.

Finishing the hillside called for illusion—plain old trickery, if you please. Due to a narrow space, the slope of the hill came out much too

steep. To visually flatten it out, I piled brush and grass higher and deeper on its bottom third. Although the steep slope is still there, its apparent angle was decreased, making the hill appear more natural.

The first layer of vegetation on

the hill is patches of spray-painted poly fiber, but the final appearance is determined by the larger fibers of synthetic steel wool and scouring pads. Those I painted with tones of olive drab, tan or sand, and brown to get a dead-grass effect. I pulled the pads into thin, ragged-edged patches, dipped them in white glue, and stuck them on the hill.

The tall yellow grass at the front of the hill is from the seedhead of full-size bottle or foxtail grass (Setaria) which grows wild across the country. If you can't find it, Woodland Scenics Field Grass looks the same.

The fallen leaves under the big tree are the brown flakes of Bruton's snuff. It must be dried in the oven because it comes in a moist cake form. I poured the dried snuff on a sheet of paper and blew it in the area under the tree, which I had squirted with diluted

Gluing photos of structures to cardboard and layering them near the backdrop makes it easy to add an entire town in a tight space.

white glue. I glued in a few sprigs of peppergrass to simulate the bushes and small trees and then sprayed the whole hill with Dullcote to secure loose fibers.

I brushed the railroad fill with white glue and covered it with screened soil and cinder ballast, but the scale-size cinders didn't look rough enough. While cleaning the gutters on my house I found the solution: grit from black asphalt shingles, each particle larger and more irregular than scale cinders. I sifted it through window screen and glued it to the fill, letting the big particles roll down the slope as on a real fill.

Coal town with building flats

With flats you can show a town or mountain and give the illusion of depth in a small space. Such was the case here, where my main line was just 4" from the wall.

Because flats can be arranged in rows, the visual and spatial relationship between them changes as the viewer moves. The trick is to arrange flats so the end of each row can't be seen, or to mask the ends with trees or another flat.

I glued pictures of structures to cardstock using contact cement, then glued 1 x 2 blocks to their backs so they would stand up. The flats rest on the back edge of the benchwork in three rows, the closest being a church, a house, and commercial buildings. Behind them is a row of houses, and the third row is a photo enlargement of a mountain and mining operation in Pennsylvania. The trees in front of the flats partially mask the town and push it back visually.

Materials such as 3M synthetic steel wool and nylon scouring pads have enough texture to represent brambles and brush as seen on the lower embankment.

For a kicker, I put in among the flats a non-detailed model of a church with an onion dome steeple, characteristic of the area. The steeple and culm banks (slate and waste coal) behind the town are key elements in the scene that would help locate it for those familiar with this part of the state.

After the scene was done, I had a visitor who grew up in the Pennsylvania anthracite region. Although I pointed out the town was strictly generic, he was willing to bet it was either Hazleton or Girardville, he wasn't sure which.

Anyone for a million bucks?

Disguising backdrop openings

Clever solutions make a layout appear larger

BY BOB SMAUS
PHOTOS BY THE AUTHOR

The main line on my HO Southern Pacific in Los Angeles layout passes though the backdrop in four different spots. I was able to squeeze a lot more visual interest out of my rather simple layout by using these transition areas to my advantage. In fact, visitors must stare intently at the layout before they figure out that the trains are simply going around in circles. Instead, trains seem to be going somewhere, vanishing from sight for at least a moment.

My first attempt at disguising a backdrop pass-through appeared on the cover of the March 1999 issue of *Model Railroader*. I used a rural highway overpass between low hills to hide the hole cut in the hardboard backdrop. It's especially convincing because if you look

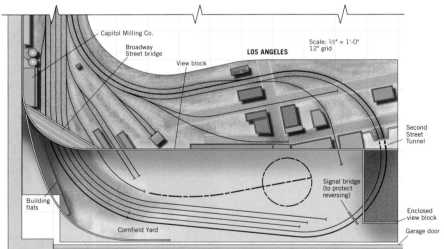

under the highway overpass, you see more hillside, unaware that this little section of hill is just for effect and is located behind the backdrop.

Another cutout on the layout was simply hidden by a Southern Pacific-style concrete tunnel portal, since mountains were part of the scenery in this spot.

But my other two pass-throughs were going to be a little more difficult to conceal—they would take some ingenuity. The following photos show what I did. They'll hopefully provide you with inspiration for your own layout—to make holes in the backdrop look as if they lead somewhere.

Solution 1
A downtown tunnel

My first troublesome pass-through is in the industrial heart of downtown Los Angeles. And I confess, the Southern Pacific had no tunnels in downtown Los Angeles. But its subsidiary, the Pacific Electric, did.

I found photos of the distinctly half-round PE tunnel portals that cut though Bunker Hill, and one showed a parking lot directly on top of the tunnel. How L.A.! Who could resist modeling that? Armed with my newfound knowledge, I blasted a tunnel though the backdrop in the most urban area of my layout.

I built a little piece of Los Angeles' famous Bunker Hill and used signs and buildings to obscure the fact that it ended so abruptly at the backdrop. One billboard advertises Greyhound Lines. Leave it to the bus company to put up a sign advertising bus service next to the railroad right-of-way!

How-to

The portal and its wings were cast of dental plaster in a wood mold, which I cut lines into to represent the form boards. I tried not to do too good a job since the real ones were lumpy and crude. I formed Bunker Hill with plaster and scenicked it.

Rather than let people look though the tunnel, I covered its back side with a wooden box that acts as a view and light block. I have room for it behind the backdrop because on the other side is staging. When the garage door is closed, there's no way to reach this part of the layout, so the illusion is successful.

To model a tunnel through Bunker Hill, Bob built up the area with scrap plywood, which he then covered with plaster.

He then added ground foam scenery and a parking lot on top.

Solution 2
Yard under a bridge

In my second, and more complex, backdrop pass-through, an entire yard had to slip unnoticed through a hardboard backdrop of painted blue sky!

My plan was to conceal this gaping hole with a yard-spanning bridge. The now-gone yard I'm modeling in downtown Los Angeles was, in fact, crossed by the wide Broadway Street bridge.

I figured the yard could look really long if it went though the backdrop and curved out of sight so you would not be able to see the end. I built a facade of urban buildings behind the backdrop, next to the yard, which would be visible under the bridge.

These simple tricks—hiding the end of the yard tracks and making it possible to look under the bridge—are extremely effective.

It appears that there's no backdrop, just rust-colored tracks stretching off into the distance with hazy blue sky overhead.

Trials

To make sure this idea would work, I dummied up the bridge using pieces of plywood. I wanted to experiment with different ways of putting scenery on the other side of the backdrop. I also had to figure out just the right height and shape for the bridge.

The illusion worked for most people, but one 6'-8" friend could see the paved top of the bridge, which destroys the illusion because the top is cut on a curve to fit into the curving backdrop.

The big arching sheet of styrene that makes up the underside of the bridge passes though the hole in the backdrop so it appears completely normal to children seeing it from a lower angle.

Cityscape

The scene I created on the other side of the backdrop is quite simple, just a few buildings and more sky painted on a short piece of curving backdrop. I discovered that this isolated bit of sky has to be lit exactly like the main section, so the two skies appear to become one.

During my experimenting, I also realized that the buildings glimpsed

under the bridge couldn't be taller than the bridge or you'd notice that their tops were chopped off by the front backdrop.

All these discoveries show why it's a good idea to mock up scenes on a layout before making them permanent.

Building bridges

Making the bridge was not difficult. From a cardboard mock-up I traced the arching bridge shape onto plywood. I used scraps of 2 x 4 and plywood to flesh out the bridge and to make it sturdy.

Then I laminated .020" styrene to the wood with Weldbond, a powerful white glue. To make the arching underside I bent another big sheet of styrene and cemented it under the sides, later trimming it to fit.

The basic bridge is really a crude model, though what it lacks in finesse, it makes up in size—it's three feet wide!

I added more layers of styrene to mimic the poured-in-place look of the real Broadway Street bridge, a monolithic concrete structure.

Disappearing act

On my layout, though not in real life, one end of the bridge disappears behind the tall buildings of Capitol Milling. The two are actually several blocks apart. A few extra utility poles in this corner also help hide the bridge's disappearance behind the building.

The other end of the bridge fades from sight behind another, less eye-catching building and a palm tree.

Here Bob test-fit the bridge before covering the plywood with styrene. He made the bridge removable, so he can weather it or add other details later on.

This photo clearly demonstrates why Bob lit the area behind the backdrop. Without the illumination, the trains disappear into a black hole, ruining the illusion.

Tips & Techniques

29 The magic of illusion

A practical guide to making your layout look larger

BY SAM POSEY
PHOTOS BY DAVE FRARY

I once started out to build the Rockies on a 4 x 8-foot sheet of plywood! Of course it couldn't be done. To model even a single mile of actual, real life terrain in HO scale takes a whopping 66 feet!

To have all the stuff we dream of—the bridges, towns, yards, and more—in some coherent arrangement, we must resort to illusion, devising ways to create an image that's more than the sum of its parts. Pulling off a successful visual illusion means harnessing the imagination and making the observer interpret "correct" sensory inputs in a different way.

Behind the scenes

This chapter explores some of the illusions that have worked best for me. My sketches overprinted on Dave Frary's photos render the concepts graphically.

I built the layout in partnership with my friend Rolf Schneider. Our concept was to invent a mythical extension of the real Colorado Midland RR. The Midland, begun in 1887, was the first standard gauge railroad to cross the Rocky Mountains. In 1918 it went bankrupt. Rolf and I like to think that had our extension connecting the Midland with the Santa Fe actually been built, Colorado cattle and ore could have reached broader markets, and the Midland could have been saved.

What's real?

Is a 6"-long HO locomotive "real?" It runs down the tracks and can pull cars; in that sense it is real. But it is shaped like a locomotive 87 times larger, which it is meant to evoke; in that sense it is an illusion. Similarly, model trees cast real shadows and model bridges work just like the real thing, even if the rivers they span are made of Enviro-Tex.

The most fundamental tool of the modeler, then, is also the most obvious: scale change. Confronted with something that is just 1/87 the size of the real thing, the viewer quickly grasps that what is "real" is the illusion. Now the modeler has a potent tool working for him, the viewer's imagination. From childhood on, we enjoy the worlds of fantasy and make-believe. Furthermore, the human brain helps by filling in a lot things that are not actually there.

The world of illusion

I've barely scratched the surface. Renaissance painters discovered the illusion of depth is organized around a loosely applied system of scale, atmospheric color, and perspective. Mirrors and special lighting have worked magic in the hands of John Allen, Malcolm Furlow, and others. With sound the newest addition to our illusionist's kit, seeing is believing—and hearing is too.

Stepping into the picture

We all know that a successful scene needs something that draws you into it and then other elements to move your eye around. The familiar formula for creating the illusion of depth is to have the eye see things that appear to be nearby, then other things far away, thus moving in and out rather than across the picture.

In this scene most people see the yellow house first, then move back to the locomotive, then forward to the man leading the horse. Once you establish the basic visual mechanics of the scene, you can tinker with the scale, color, and texture to strengthen the sense of depth. Here, the scale changes drastically from the large foreground pine to a distant town made up of buildings about 1″ long on the ridge above the locomotive. You can barely make one of them out here.

To further enhance the illusion of distance, the color changes from warm foreground earth tones to cool distant blues and greens. There's plenty of texture in the foreground rocks and shingles, while the distant mountains are just thin acrylic washes on smooth plaster.

Accenting the vertical

There is nothing subtle about this shot! Extreme vertical space, emphasized by the narrowness and frailty of the bridge support, is this view's primary dynamic, but it is balanced by the way the river takes the eye straight back into the center.

Without reliable references such as buildings and trees, scale change can be created abstractly. A series of rectangles, diminishing in size, moves the eye back into the picture.

Each rectangle is keyed to a notch in the cliff that runs up the right side of the picture. The largest is bounded on the right by the lowest notch in the cliff, the deep shadow on the rocks to the far left, and the bridge across the top. See it?

The next rectangle is the gap under the bridge, with the lower right-hand corner marked by the notch right across from the base of the bridge support. The last is the dark area at the end of the river. The rectangles are like a series of doors leading you in.

Forcing the perspective

When we imagine rails stretching out to the horizon we think (correctly) that the horizon is far away. Now, when we see rails intersecting in the distance, our experience is ready to tell us that they are meeting at the horizon.

I designed this yard so that the main line sweeping in from the left intersects with the convergence of the yard tracks and creates a false vanishing point. This establishes a "horizon" much closer than it really would be, thereby driving everything behind it even farther away.

Space as time

In this scene we're creating space in a way entirely different from the others. The essence of the tableau is narrative: A locomotive has derailed and obviously there is a story here.

"Space" takes the form of the interval of time between the moment of the wreck (probably last night, when this mountain pass was shrouded in mist) and when the Midland's staff photographer, Big Man Dave, eased down the cliff with his heavy equipment to take the photo.

When people visit my layout, they see the wreck of old number 18 and invariably ask when it happened. Whether it actually ever "happened" at all simply isn't brought into question. Seeing is believing.

Close but far away

Here we see what can be done to make two essentially parallel tracks inhabit different worlds. This scene has two kinds of space in tension. In the foreground, the bridge creates a concave space, while the background space is convex, bending around a hill. The deep chasm between the trains makes them seem farther apart.

Going to our scale/color/texture bag, the bridge's height contrasts with the scaled down trees in the background, the girders' warm color contrasts with cool shadows playing across the mountains, and Rolf's detailing of the bridge pulls it forward, while the distant trees are further diminished by being clumped together.

Slowing for curves

This scene illustrates how an S bend can expand space. Imagine how the scene would look if the track ran straight from the locomotive back to the caboose—the distance between them would seem less, right? But because the eye must swing right, left, right as it follows the S, it moves more slowly than if it were just connecting two points. The extra time sends a signal the brain interprets as greater distance.

I wanted to slow the eye movement even further, so I created a second, backward, S out of the bare rocks, a visual obstruction that subtly suggests the train is fighting its way through the scenery.

90

The suggestion of more

In this scene a diagonal slices across the picture, inviting the viewer to stroll up the main street. This is a busy scene, but much of what you think is in it is only partly there, with the rest left to the imagination—the same way seeing the corner of a table at the edge of a picture infers that the rest of the table exists. Here crowding the buildings together suggests more town—but there isn't.

A whole train is suggested by a glimpse of two coaches, and the viewer's knowledge that they must be sitting on a track creates an implied horizontal which leads the eye to the station on the left. The land office sign, perhaps missed at first, reminds the viewer that beyond the town, unseen but very much there, are the broad sunlit plains of Colorado.

30 Forced perspective
Using structures and scenery to create the illusion of distance

BY EARL SMALLSHAW
PHOTOS BY THE AUTHOR

There's an old saying that you can never be too thin or too rich. For model railroaders, I would add that you can never have too much space. However, in planning a layout, almost everyone is confronted by the lack of space, so we must make the best use of what we have.

Forced perspective is a modeling technique used to fit structures and scenery into a shallow space while adding depth to a scene. Perspective, simply put, means that objects close to you appear larger than those farther away. In modeling we can force this illusion by reducing the size of background structures and trees to make them seem more distant than they actually are (fig. 1).

To make a successful forced perspective scene, it's important that you follow these three principles:
• Structures in the extreme background should have little or no detail, because when looking at a structure in the distance you can't make out much detail. The structures' colors should be muted and neutral so as not to attract attention.
• For the same reason make the color of the scenery in the background lighter and more muted.
• Detail and color intensity of structures and scenery should increase accordingly toward the front to draw the viewer's eye to the foreground of the scene.

The town of Mystic on my HO scale layout is located in a shallow corner. I built the foreground structures in town full size; the forced perspective began behind the shops.

Here is the town of Mystic on Earl Smallshaw's HO layout. Smaller-than-scale structures and trees in the background add apparent depth to this shallow scene.

Fig. 1 PERSPECTIVE. The two-sided structure in the foreground is full HO size. The next three are cardboard mockups, each progressively smaller. Although these models seem far apart, there's less than ½" between each structure, demonstrating forced perspective.

Fig. 2 BACKGROUND BUILDINGS. Earl's background structures are made of styrene. This one, about 1" square and 1¼" high, is the most distant structure in his scene. There is no attempt to add detail, and the neutral color won't attract attention.

Building and positioning structures

All of my background structures are made of styrene. They are simple boxes with windows cut in and a roof (see fig. 2). A short piece of square styrene serves as a chimney. I apply no detail to these structures.

With the scenery base already in place, I measure the distance from the back of the foreground structure to the point where the most distant structure will be positioned, in this case 5". Don't become carried away and make the distant structure too small. For example, in this scene my most distant structure is about 1" square and 1¼" high.

Distant structures are best positioned on a hillside, slightly above the foreground ones. Ensure that each distant structure doesn't lean, as leaning buildings will be very noticeable.

Once I'm satisfied with the position of the structure, I glue it in place. I use plaster to fill in gaps between the structure's foundation and the scenery base. I glue small bits of Woodland Scenics ground foam around the foundation.

Next I construct the background structures closest to the full-sized foreground structures. These are reduced in size 10 to 20 percent.

The house behind Kate's Cafe measures 1¼" x 1½" x 2¼" high and is set on a shelf to ease the transition from the foreground to the background (fig. 3). The detail is more evident here because the house is closer to the foreground.

The next house (¾" x 1¼" x 1¾" high) was mounted on a pedestal to enable me to position this structure at the correct angle and height to blend into the background scene (also fig. 3).

Adding foliage

Once all buildings are in place, stand back and view the scene from different angles. If you're satisfied that the perspective is correct, then add foliage to provide distance and separation for depth.

The first foliage to consider is the trees and branches between the foreground structures and the first background structures. Squeeze in some parts of trees to disguise the fact that the two structures are so close. Hang branches over the roof of the foreground structure to break up straight edges.

Continue inserting foliage around the other background structures, keeping trees in proportion to the decreasing size of the structures (fig. 4). If you think the colors of the background structures and scenery are too intense, use an airbrush to slightly mist the scene. I sparingly apply a diluted mix of Floquil Grime (two parts thinner to one part paint).

Creating a forced perspective background scene isn't difficult and can give the appearance of more depth than you actually have. Give it a try!

Fig. 3 POSITIONING. One house rests on a shelf behind Kate's Cafe. This was done to position the structure at the right elevation for the background scene. The other house is mounted on a wood pedestal. Structures mounted in this way are easily repositioned to achieve the best look.

Fig. 4 FOLIAGE. It's important to keep bushes and trees in proportion to the surrounding houses. Here Earl used Woodland Scenics turf around the foundation. A small branch cut from a foreground tree (left) serves as the tree in the yard of this background house.

31 Two scenes for the space of one

A mirror and other modeling tricks to make the layout look larger

BY DAVE BIGGE
PHOTOS BY THE AUTHOR

No matter how much room we have for our trains, it's never enough. We're always compromising or using illusion to squeeze in more railroad or make what we have look larger. I'm going to describe my solution to one of the challenges I faced on my layout, then tell how I went about building the actual scenes. You probably will not want to copy this section of my railroad exactly, but I hope the methods might be helpful in imagineering your own pike.

Let me set the scene. I'm basing my layout on the prototype Rio Grande Southern, a 3-foot-gauge railroad that operated from the 1890s until the early 1950s in southwestern Colorado. The RGS was 160 miles long and interchanged with the Denver & Rio Grande Western at both ends. I'm modeling the northern division only (Ridgway to Rico) with lots of compression and poetic license. Some scenes are based on the prototype, while others are free-lanced. The scenes described in this chapter are free-lanced, but I tried to get the feeling of the actual railroad into them. I model in Sn3, that is S scale (³⁄₁₆″ = 1 foot), narrow gauge (3 feet between the rails). My layout is built in my garage and is about 14 x 25 feet.

I faced a problem we all have in track planning: how to get as much distance between towns as possible. The loop between Pandora and Vance Junction (see the track plan) was one answer. Now I had to make the loop look interesting and also see if there was some way to use the space inside it for something other than just a mountain to circle around.

THE MINING SCENE Our author added a loop to his Sn3 layout to gain running room, then used the area inside it to create two major scenes, one being this mining valley. A mirror under the conveyor housing doubles the area's apparent size.

THE CANYON SCENE The ridge holding the mining scene mirror also provides a backdrop for the loop's second scene, featuring scenery descending nearly to the floor. Upper right is the tunnel from which the train will emerge in a few minutes.

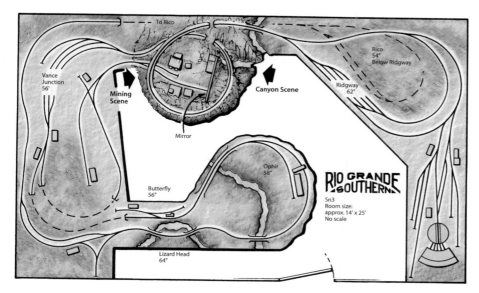

Vance
Junction
56"

To Rico

Rico
54"
Below Ridgway

Mining
Scene

Canyon Scene

Ridgway
62"

Mirror

Ophir
58"

Butterfly
56"

RIO GRANDE
SOUTHERN

Lizard Head
64"

Sn3
Room size:
approx. 14' x 25'
No scale

By running a high ridge across the loop, I could divide it into two big scenes. The first, I decided, would be a dramatic trestle soaring high above a mountain stream.

The second scene would use the loop's center to form a U-shaped valley containing a mining area to be called Pandora and to be served by a branch line from Vance Junction. To make Pandora look larger I would install a mirror at the far end.

Construction

First, I built L-girder framework to support the track and scenery; then I laid in the flat base for Pandora. For this and all the roadbed, I used ½" plywood with a layer of Homasote on top. Since the mirror's location would dictate the scenic forms both in front of and behind it, I positioned it next.

In the past I had always laid track and then built scenery, but this time I tried it the other way around and found I liked it. I fudged a little by laying flexible track on the roadbed and running some trains for awhile to check grade and curvature.

Before removing the flextrack, I made tracings of the rails where the bridges would go. These would be used as templates for constructing the bridge decks at the workbench. I carefully marked the ends of the

bridge approaches, then installed risers at those points to keep the roadbed from shifting when I cut it. Finally, I pulled up the temporary track, cut out the roadbed sections where the bridges would go, and started making scenery.

I built my scenic forms with the hardshell method, laying plaster-soaked paper towels over a temporary base of crumpled newspaper. See fig. 1. When the plaster was dry I pulled the paper out, leaving a hollow, fairly light shell. The only drawbacks to this method are that it is messy and you need a special type of plaster (Hydrocal, made by U.S. Gypsum), which I understand is hard to find in some places.

The first section I worked on was the part against the wall between Ridgway and Vance, as this area would be difficult to get at once the mountain was in place. I built most of this scenery standing in a cozy, temporary access hole.

I did not want to be able to see Pandora from the "wrong" side, so the top of the ridge behind it is 7 feet above the floor. To make the bridge at Pleasant Valley as dramatic as possible, I dropped the scenery to about 12" from the floor. I wanted to drop it all the way, but would have had a problem with foot room in the aisle.

When the hardshell was dry, I added a layer of molding plaster on

top to form the ground. Before applying this plaster I moistened the hardshell with "wet water" (water with a drop or two of liquid detergent added) so it wouldn't pull moisture from the upper layer and cause it to set too fast.

Next, I added plaster rock castings made in rubber molds purchased at hobby shops. To make the castings I first wet the mold with water, then filled it with a soupy mixture of casting plaster. When the plaster was "semi-set" I just placed the mold where I wanted my rock and formed it to the contour of the area. When the plaster was almost set and felt warm to the touch, I peeled the mold away, and presto! Instant cliffs.

Blending the seams between the castings was a little tricky. After peeling away the mold I used an old blade in a hobby knife to chip away any ooze marks. When I rubbed the seams with my finger to blend them or used a wire brush to stipple the area, the coloring I used didn't take well and left a white area. That's why I went to the chipping method, just breaking away the edges until they looked good and then letting the plaster dry thoroughly.

I also use a hobby knife to carve in stone retaining walls, which were a feature of many of the Colorado narrow gauge lines. By doing a small section at a time I can work on the plaster before it gets too hard.

After completing all the plastering I spent a fair amount of time checking the work, trying to find all my runs, drips, and voids. It's a little hard to find them because you're looking at a large expanse of white. If you miss any you can always fix them later, but it's easier to do it now. Be sure to wet the area with wet water before doing any patching.

Coloring and detailing

Next comes the fun part—coloring and detailing. These steps are

Fig. 1. BUILDING THE CANYON SCENE. Right top: The author built scenery using the hardshell method popularized by Linn Westcott. The shell is plaster-dipped paper towels over crumpled newspaper. The roadbed was in place, but the track was not yet laid. Right center: Plaster rock castings were added, as well as a stone pier to support one end of the bridge. The bridge was built at the workbench, then installed. Right bottom: Color was built up carefully, spraying on washes of earth-tone tints and water.

the reward for all the preliminary work. First, I give the white plaster ground a basic earth color by spraying or brushing on thin washes, using tinting colors available in tubes at paint stores.

I use about ½" of pigment in a pint of water with a drop of detergent mixed in. The following colors sprayed on in various combinations do the job: raw umber, burnt umber, raw sienna, burnt sienna, and lampblack. If you're not sure which colors to use, experiment on the hardshell before adding the final coat of plaster.

To use the colors I spray the raw plaster with a little wet water and then spray on the tints. For coloring ground I'm usually firing away from a spray bottle of raw umber in my right hand and one of burnt umber in my left. Rock castings get a spray of lampblack for starters, followed by sprays of the other colors as the mood strikes.

I spray some color on, then stop and let it dry. Usually it lightens, and I go back and give it another shot. I've found it's important to work up to the final color slowly because if you get the scenery too dark there's not much you can do to lighten it. I just spray until the coloring looks a little too bold, then quit. Once dry it's usually about right. Actually, using the thinned washes makes it difficult to get the color too dark unless you mix too much pigment into the water in the first place. Whenever you mix a fresh batch of color, test it before spraying finished scenery.

Nothing I've found looks more like dirt than dirt, so that's what I use. When the weather is good, I go soil prospecting and collect various shades of decomposed granite. After I get home, I dry what I've found. Later, I sift it to various textures and then store it in plastic

Fig. 2. BUILDING THE MINING SCENE. Right: The author positioned a mirror in the ridge separating the mining scene from the canyon scene. Cardboard formers established viewing angles. One mine was built against the mirror, doubling its apparent size. The forward mine was mocked up with foamcore board. Wood was later added to finish the walls. A cardboard mock-up, left, was used to determine the tipple's final position.

bags. Any dirt that will dry to a dust or flour-like texture will work. Soil with lots of clay in it will not work. If you live where the right type of soil is hard to find, you can always buy it "dirt cheap" at the closest hobby shop.

To apply the dirt, just sprinkle it where you want it, then wet the soil with wet water until it's saturated. Next, dribble on white glue diluted 50:50 with water and allow it to dry The wet soil absorbs the glue, and when it dries it looks loose, even though it isn't.

On the steeper places I brushed white glue on the surface, then misted the soil on. "Misted" is a fancy way of saying I held a card with some dirt on it in front of my mouth and blew the dirt into position.

You should vary your soil colors using the color of your rock castings as a guide. Use darker colors where moisture would be present and lighter, "drier" colors where it wouldn't. These and many more

Fig. 3. THE TRESTLE AT PANDORA. Dave first built the deck and bents for trestle guarding the mines' entrance at his workbench, then he assembled them in place.

scenery techniques are beautifully discussed in Dave Frary's book *How to Build Realistic Model Railroad Scenery* (Kalmbach Publishing Co.).

Next, I blobbed on lots of ground foam in a random manner, using several colors and textures. To secure the foam I used diluted matte medium. Lastly, I sprinkled rocks and twigs here and there and planted a few trees. I'll add more trees as time permits.

The Pandora scene

The mirror became the deciding factor in arranging the Pandora scene. See fig. 2. I had never tried the mirror trick before and worked by trial-and-error, constantly checking how things looked directly as well as how they looked in the mirror.

This is not a huge area, only about 2½ x 4 feet, so other tricks were employed to make it look larger, starting with the "half-building" mill positioned against the

mirror to make it look twice as large as it actually is.

To force the perspective a little, I built both the half mill and the conveyor hiding the top of the mirror in HO. (Remember, I model in S scale, which is larger than HO.) The idea was to make the buildings appear farther from the viewer than they really are. The difference in scale is not readily apparent, but I decided not to run any track to the HO mill so the viewer wouldn't be able to compare sizes.

Next, I built a large S scale mill for the other side of the valley. I first made a mock-up, using foam-core board (an art supply store item), and then cutting the board and taping it together in several configurations until I was happy with the design.

To construct the building I used the foamcore as subwalls and covered them with board-and-batten siding, made by gluing on individual 2 x 12 boards and 1 x 2 battens. Those parts of the building that can be seen only in the mirror I painted boxcar red rather than the raw wood of the forward sides. This made the building in the mirror look subtly different from the real one.

Once the mine was completed I worked the scenery up around it so it looked as if it were built into the hillside. Some rock castings were added at the far end of the canyon because the mountain there had to be nearly vertical and cliffs seemed the logical choice.

On the left side of the valley I wanted a spur and loading tipple. I built a cardboard mock-up and tried several locations. Placing it on the hillside allowed me to nar-row the valley at the entrance and hide some distracting reflections in the mirror. The long bridge, shown in fig. 3, also helps the scene's real-ism. It doesn't permit a wide-open view, making it difficult to detect tricks like the mirror and under-sized buildings.

I hope you enjoyed this story and picked up a tidbit or two. The best way to start building scenery is just do it. It's fun and inexpensive, so if you decide later you could have done part of it better, just grab the old hammer, bash it out, and do it again.

32 It's the little things that count
Careful attention to detail makes scenes come alive

BY MICHAEL TYLICK
PHOTOS BY THE AUTHOR

George Sellios has built one of the most delightful model railroads of recent times. Aside from the vastness and artistry of the completed city portion of the HO scale Franklin & South Manchester (featured in the March 1990 *Model Railroader),* one of the things I enjoy most is George's careful attention to the smallest details.

His city of Manchester abounds with hundreds of small, everyday events and stories—so many that the eye flits from one to the next. The effect is much like looking out the window of a train: tiny slices of life flash by to be quickly digested and replaced by the next.

Photos isolating very small areas of the F&SM are truly the best way to appreciate the attention lavished on every square inch of this enormous layout. Although the F&SM is a very large private layout, all the scenes here could fit on even the smallest layouts.

The A. Zol Co. is an interesting structure. The tall square tower with its hip roof and finial looks like it originally had a different use. We can only surmise what it was. George has left to our imagination what A. Zol actually makes, but, judging by the many wood barrels and crates, their product looks small but heavy. The forklift, hand trucks, and wagons are needed to move them. Judging by the number of roof vents and ductwork, it also appears they deal with many toxic or dusty materials. Instead of a "one-of-each" type of platform clutter, George has wisely made most of the packing look similar: after all, a small industry has a limited product line. But a scale, a few oil drums, and some trash barrels give some variety to the scene.

The placement of the figures is also nicely done. A number of people are clustered on the main platform. The man with the cowboy hat, perhaps the foreman, appears to be discussing a problem with the workers, who are obviously on a break. The break is the problem, and the man just above the rail bumper has decided he'd better look busy, while the worker at the far left either didn't get the message yet or else figures he's safely out of view. Across the tracks, there are many more figures and vehicles telling their own stories. One of the greatest joys in visiting the F&SM is that the areas three feet away from the aisle are just as intensely detailed as the foreground.

George has been wise to treat different parts of the scene differently. Variations in coloring, scale (size of structures), signs, and rooflines make this a photo that can be studied for hours, with new lessons to be learned with every look.

The vitality of a city is its street life. Although thousands of people may live and work in the large buildings, the street is where they interact with each other. In the days before many central cities became ghettos, people from all walks of life mixed together on the streets. During the Depression, with so many fortunes lost and so many people out of work, the groupings became even more eclectic.

One also notices the many vehicles. George has been accused of overly crowding the streets with cars, trucks, and buses, but have you ever tried to cross a downtown city street? Although there's a great variety of automobiles (I'd like to know where he found them all!), he's managed to keep the colors muted and dark, a relief from Ford basic black, but not the rainbow of color found in a contemporary parking lot. A horse and wagon are also at work. By this time they are becoming much less common in the city than a decade or two earlier, even if horsepower was still prevalent in rural areas.

The alley shows the large variety of junk thrown there. Even these hidden areas have their own stories. Notice how the cracks, the repairs, the differences of surfaces of the streets are so much more interesting than a plain piece of gray Masonite. The streetlights are dif-

ferent, having been installed or replaced at different times. The trash cans and old newspapers complete the scene.

Every inch of this city has something to look at. I've never subscribed to the school of thought of selectively detailing certain areas, leaving the viewer to skip over "blank" areas. It may save some time, but George's method makes his layout much more fun to look at. George has filled a large space with so many fascinating things to observe that I find it surprising so few modelers, even those with small layouts, have detailed them to the same intensity.

Everything looks new and active on many model railroads. Many of us forget to show signs of neglect. Industrial structures outlive their usefulness and are often left to decay. Here we have a loading dock (an Alexander kit) that has been forgotten. The track to it is weed-grown and rusted. Even the rail tops are dirty, showing that model freight cars don't go there anymore.

A few barrels have been left around, and a good number of the floorboards have been scavenged by the hoboes that frequent this part of town. Weeds have grown up through the open places, and the access road looks barely passable. The column from a hoist has been left, but the crane itself has been removed for use elsewhere. The vacant lot around the dock is also pretty barren, but the use of many colors and textures has made this area interesting. The factories in the rear, with their crowded and bustling shipping areas, lend an even greater contrast to the dirt and desolation.

George is smart to keep changing the treatments of similar surfaces in his scenes. Note the many different styles of pavement on the streets and sidewalks, as well as the way a road is made interesting with defects and the attempts to repair them. Fewer people and cars populate this destitute part of town, where the greatest activity seems to be the passing of a train. The long, curved turnout with its frog in the middle of a grade crossing is a typical city sight, as not all parts of the city are separated from the railroad by bridges.

Although most model city scenes are built on flat pieces of plywood, George has chosen to add depth to his city. Even a small foreground area in front of the tracks can be multi-leveled. Tracks are often elevated or depressed in congested areas to avoid traffic tie-ups, and in this instance the F&SM main line is above street level.

Usually forgotten are the many utility systems beneath our feet. If the earth were transparent, the work underneath would be almost as interesting and complicated to model as what we see. George has suggested the existence of this underground world with a small repair excavation in a dirt parking lot. Aside from the construction details, I find the treatment of the dirt particularly interesting. The variety of textures in the parking lot is delightful. Not just the ruts; there are areas that look hard and soft, areas that weeds have taken over, and of course the dirt (it even gets darker in the hole) that was dug up.

Many other things are also going on in this small scene. The industrial paraphernalia has been piled along the walls to make room for digging. Business still goes on, so the construction crew must work around the workers' automobiles. Over in the left corner one man appears to be changing a flat tire, no doubt caused by the construction debris. On the upper level, the by-products of another industry are in evidence, as is the worker by the railing (in a city all walls have railings) taking a break and nonchalantly watching the excavation.

An evergreen tree frames the scene nicely. In an older city, there is much more wild foliage than many of us realize. Notice how carefully George has removed the gloss from everything. I didn't notice this particular scene until George pointed it out. I'm glad he did; it's a wonderful little piece of reality that could be a real showpiece on almost any layouts.

Useful addresses

Your local hobby shop is typically the best place to look for scenery products, tools, and materials, but here are current addresses for the manufacturers of some of the special items mentioned in this book.

Accurate Dimensionals
4185 S Fox Street
Englewood, CO 80110-4564
(303) 762-0460

AMSI
P.O. Box 750638
Petaluma, CA 94975
(707) 763-6000
www.AMSI-minilandscaping.com
E-mail: macamsi@svn.net

Dremel
4915 21st Street
Racine, WI 53406
(262) 554-1390
Toll-free: (800) 437-3635

Envirotex (product)
P.O. Box 365
Fields Landing, CA 95337
(707) 443-9323

Floquil-Polly S Color Corp
(see Testor)

Michaels
1721 Montgomery Hwy. S
Hoover, AL 35244
(705) 733-8067

Microscale Industries
18435 Bandilier Circle
Fountain Valley, CA 92708
(714) 593-1422
Toll-free: (800) 722-5306

Plastruct
1020 S Wallace Place
City of Industry, CA 91748
(626) 912-7016
Toll-free: (800) 666-7015
www.plastruct.com
E-mail: plastruct@aol.com

The Testor Corp.
620 Buckbee Street
Rockford, IL 61104
(815) 962-6654
Toll-free: (800) 962-6654
www.testors.com
E-mail: testors@testors.com

Vintage Reproductions
2606 Flintridge Drive
Colorado Springs, CO 80918-4408
(719) 598-2274
E-mail: hume@compuserve.com

Wm K. Walthers Inc.
5601 W Florist Avenue
P.O. Box 3039
Milwaukee, WI 53201-3039
(414) 527-0770
Toll-free: (800) 877-7171
www.walthers.com
E-mail:
newaccounts@walthers.com

Woodland Scenics
101 East Valley Drive
P.O. Box 98
Linn Creek, MO 65052
(573) 346-5555
www.woodlandscenics.com
E-mail:
sales@woodlandscenics.com